45-46 } TEST
50-51

D0204175

*Harmony
and Ear Training
at the Keyboard*

Harmony
and Ear Training
at the Keyboard

Fourth Edition

Stanley Shumway

School of Fine Arts
University of Kansas

THE LIBRARY
UNIVERSITY OF SAINT FRANCIS
WITHDRAWN
2701 SPRING STREET
FORT WAYNE, INDIANA 46808

wcb

Wm. C. Brown Publishers
Dubuque, Iowa

Consulting Editor

Frederick W. Westphal
California State University, Sacramento

Copyright © 1970, 1976, 1980, 1984 by
Wm. C. Brown Company Publishers. All rights reserved

Library of Congress Catalog Card Number: 79–55151

ISBN 0–697–03618–9

No part of this publication may be reproduced, stored in a
retrieval system, or transmitted, in any form or by any means,
electronic, mechanical, photocopying, recording, or otherwise,
without the prior written permission of the publisher.

Printed in the United States of America
10 9 8 7 6 5 4 3 2

2   03618   01

Contents

Preface

The keyboard harmony class can be among the most valuable learning experiences in a music theory curriculum. Our study of music is essentially reliant on the symbolic system of music notation. Analysis, composition, part-writing, sight-reading, and dictation are all important processes which depend on the visual medium; and yet the single most vital musical skill is hearing. The special value of the keyboard class lies in the fact that it minimizes the need for visual representation while maximizing the opportunities for aural experience. Here concepts can be illustrated, examined, and evaluated spontaneously in terms of musical sound, without necessarily translating the sound to symbols. The keyboard class offers unique opportunities for sound-to-sound comparisons—for instance, the perceived difference between two performed passages. Direct dictation, or "instant replay", is a beneficial exercise in which a phrase or harmonic progression is dictated by one person and played back by another. To the extent that notation is used, there are continuing opportunities in class for critical comparisons between sight and sound —notation and performance.

All that is required as preparation for this program of study is an understanding of the fundamentals of tonal music—rhythm and meter, intervals, scales and key signatures. Some familiarity with the piano keyboard is also desirable, although well developed performing proficiency is not essential. At the University of Kansas students are required to have at least one semester of piano study before beginning the four-semester keyboard harmony curriculum. It is sometimes assumed that keyboard harmony is too difficult for college students, but this view is not supported by the experience at this and other universities. The degree of challenge in this study is relative to the quantity of work assigned and to the qualitative expectations for class performance. Some students easily prepare all the exercises in a project, others may be able to master only a few selected problems, but the learning benefits are substantial in both cases. Playing at a rapid tempo is not necessary; indeed, the learning values are probably enhanced by more deliberate performance. Harmonic progression can be perceived even in very slow tempos if a regular pulse is maintained.

Keyboard classes can be held in rooms with one piano, or with several. When multiple pianos are available there is increased opportunity for more rapid exchanges and musical dialogues. When a single piano is used it is possible to have two players at the keyboard. The primary activity in a keyboard class, besides the playing itself, is constant and careful listening. Students follow the performances of their peers and identify content, errors, etc. The paper keyboards at the back of the book may be used for silent monitoring of a performed exercise. Writing, at a chalkboard or on paper, is a valuable supplemental activity, and it is often desirable to thereby freeze a passage for further scrutiny. Generally, however, it is advised that exercises assigned for keyboard realization should not be written out in advance. The unique value of this program results from renewed concentration on a problem each time it is performed, and this value is diminished when an exercise is written out and memorized.

This book contains a series of projects, arranged progressively, which are designed to demonstrate the principles of harmony from diatonic triads through chromatic harmony and twentieth century practices. Most of the projects are based on a three-part format: (1) typical settings of a given chord, (2) phrases with figured bass in which the chord is employed in a variety of contexts, and (3) melody harmonization, again emphasizing the chord under consideration. These three activities progress generally from easier to more difficult, and each builds upon the preceding exercises. Thus, the typical harmonic-melodic settings reappear in the figured bass phrases and are included again in the melodies for harmonization.

Throughout the book there are repeated reminders to listen critically while performing—to sing along with the bass notes or chord roots, to imagine sounds before playing, etc. The importance of this mental-aural exercise cannot be over-emphasized. Concentration and diligence are required, and it is suggested that practice is most efficient when carried on in daily sessions of 30 minutes or less.

Stanley N. Shumway
Lawrence, Kansas
1983

Unit I
The Diatonic Triads

Keyboard Orientation

The versatility of the piano makes it indispensable for musicians, not only as a performing medium, but also as an everyday tool for use in study, composition, and analysis. The piano enables us to communicate musical thoughts by spontaneously transforming notation or ideas into sound. Performers, teachers, conductors, scholars, and composers all make frequent use of the instrument.

It is this utilitarian function of the piano which is developed in this book. The primary focus is on harmony: chords, their structure, relationships, and operations in a musical context. The piano keyboard enables us to test hypotheses and to bring theoretical concepts to life. This testing, vitalizing process is dependent upon acute aural discrimination. Throughout the book there are repeated admonitions to listen intently to the sounds played and to try to recall and to imagine how chords sound.

The physical dexterity required in this study is minimal, since the piano is relatively simple to operate in a functional role. It is important, however, to concurrently develop your powers of mental and aural concentration, and many of the exercises which follow are designed to cultivate these abilities.

Pitch Matching

One of the most basic of aural skills is the ability to mentally and vocally match any pitch that you hear. Here are some suggestions to help you cultivate this important skill. In the following exercises the diamond-shaped notes represent pitches to be sung.

1. Play a note in your vocal range and sing it back ("la") as quickly as possible. Listen very carefully for accuracy of pitch. Focus mentally before singing so that you begin precisely on the pitch rather than with a sliding approach.

2. Gradually extend this technique by playing notes in higher and lower registers and mentally transposing the necessary octaves to sing the pitch in your voice range. The problem soon becomes more challenging as you extend the range and play the notes in more rapid succession.

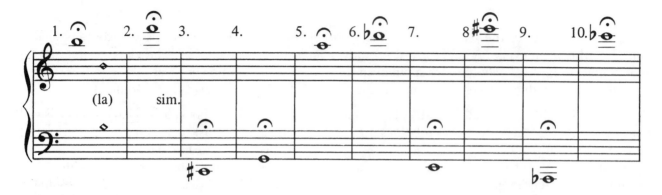

3. Play melodic patterns of two or three notes and sing them back. Again, the range may be systematically extended.

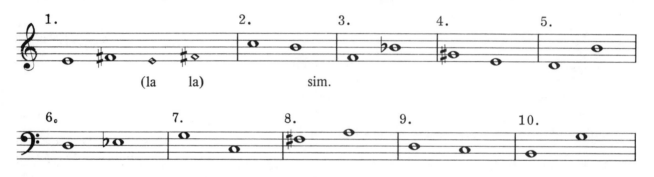

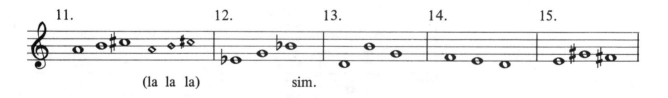

4. Play two notes simultaneously, using one finger of each hand, and sing them back, beginning with either the lower or higher pitch. Try this in several registers and with varying distances between the notes.

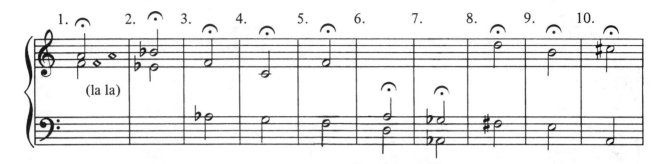

5. The reverse of this type of drill is to sing before playing. Establish a reference pitch by playing a note in your vocal range. Sing another pitch, either higher or lower, and then play the key that will match the sung pitch. Do this also with short melodic patterns.

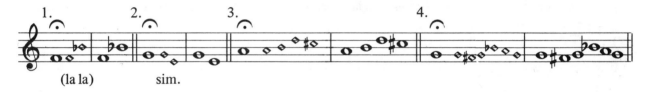

Five-Finger Position

1. Play the first five notes of major and minor scales, up and down, first with each hand alone and then with both together in various octaves. Each pattern will utilize the five fingers in consecutive order. For example:

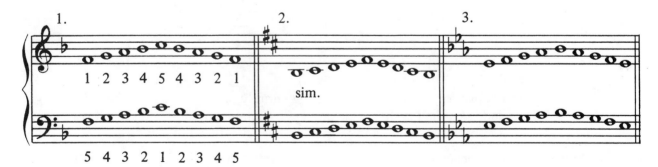

2. Now sing the same patterns using *scale degree* numbers: 1-2-3-4-5-4-3-2-1. Play the tonic note before singing, and play the entire pattern after, to test your intonation. Listen especially to the third scale degree that distinguishes major from minor in these patterns.

1 2 3 4 5 4 3 2 1

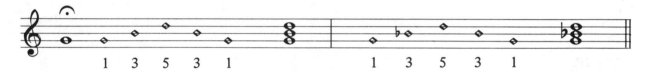

1 2 3 4 5 4 3 2 1

3. To further develop this major-minor awareness, sing and play triad patterns: 1-3-5-3-1. Play a reference tone, sing both types of triads using the given tone as the root, and play the triads.

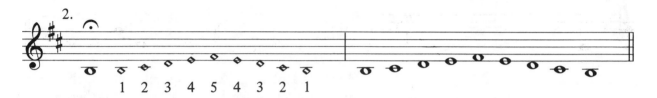

1 3 5 3 1   1 3 5 3 1

4. Also try using the given pitch as the third or fifth of a major or minor triad. Sing the given note with the appropriate number, then sing the root and proceed as before. The patterns will be 3-1-3-5-3-1 or 5-1-3-5-3-1.

3 1 3 5 3 1   3 1 3 5 3 1

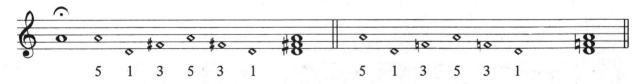

5 1 3 5 3 1   5 1 3 5 3 1

5. The exercises above employ patterns consisting entirely of either steps or skips. Create your own short melodies on the first five scale degrees by combining steps and skips. Play and echo these by singing back the scale degree numbers. Also sing first and play back.

Some melodic tendencies of the scale tones may be observed, such as: (1) the relative stability of scale degrees 1 and 3 as compared with 2 and 4, (2) the strong inclination of 4 to move to 3, and 2 to move to 1 or 3, and (3) the fundamental strength of the patterns 5-1, 4-5-1, and 2-5-1.

Here are some examples of short melodic patterns. Play, and sing scale degree numbers. Also sing without playing. These patterns all begin on the tonic, scale degree 1.

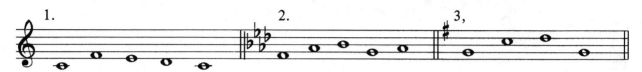

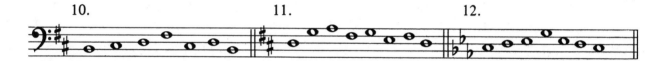

6. Think of familiar melodies that begin with melodic patterns in the first five notes of the scale. Play and sing as above. For example:

1
1
1 2 3
3 2 3 4 5
etc.

1 1 2 3   1 3 2 5   1 1 2 3   1   7 etc.

3

etc.

4.

etc.

5.

etc.

6.

etc.

Scales, Intervals, and Triads

I. Play major and minor scales, ascending and descending, with one or both hands. Sing the scale degree numbers. Keep a slow but regular tempo and listen for uniform keyboard articulation and vocal intonation. The harmonic form of minor is the most useful at this stage. Note that it differs from major only at the third and sixth scale steps.

While advanced performing dexterity at the keyboard is not essential to this study, it will be helpful to you to use logical fingering patterns. Pianists employ various fingerings depending on the black and white key configuration of the scale. The little finger is used *only* for the bottom note (left hand) and the top note (right hand) of certain scales. The other fingers and thumb play alternating groups of three and four notes.

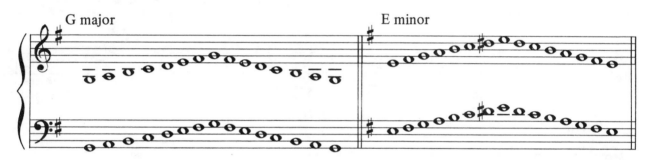

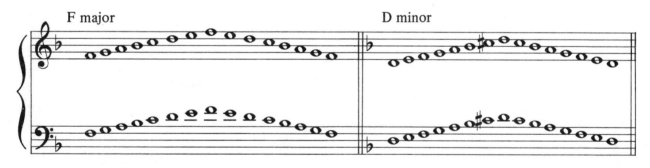

II. Sing intervals above or below a given tonic. Select and play a tonic note in your voice range, sing the tonic and another scale degree (for instance "one-five"), and check your accuracy by playing. Most of the diatonic intervals occur in this context and facility in this exercise is of considerable importance. Determine which intervals are most difficult for you and concentrate your practice on these. (Tests suggest that the intervals most commonly missed are the minor sixth and minor third.) As before, the diamond-shaped note heads are to be sung rather than played.

Ascending intervals

C major

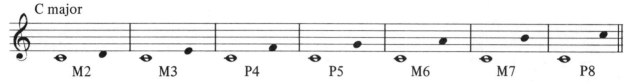

C minor

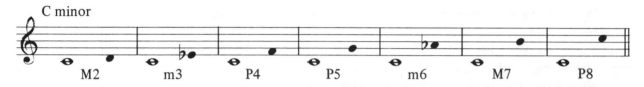

Descending intervals

C major

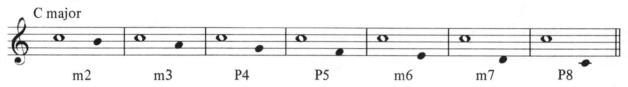

C minor

one - five   one - three

one - six   one - four

III. Play the following bass lines with the left hand. Sing the scale degree numbers as you play.

A. Major Keys.

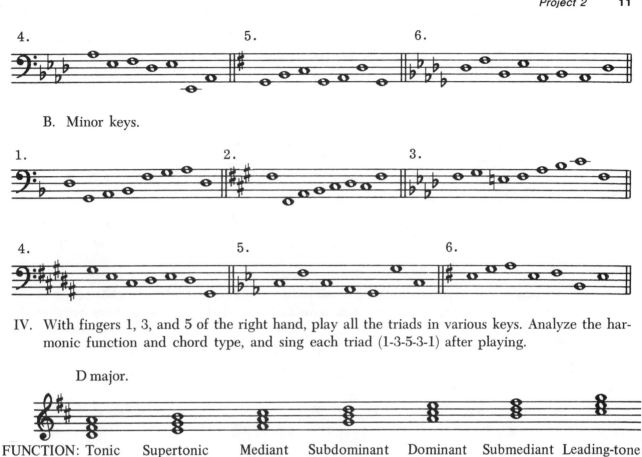

4.   5.   6.

B. Minor keys.

1.   2.   3.

4.   5.   6.

IV. With fingers 1, 3, and 5 of the right hand, play all the triads in various keys. Analyze the harmonic function and chord type, and sing each triad (1-3-5-3-1) after playing.

D major.

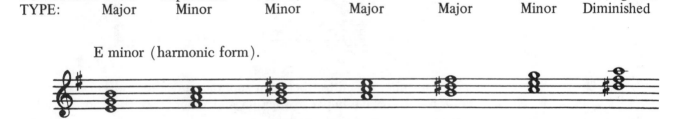

FUNCTION:	Tonic	Supertonic	Mediant	Subdominant	Dominant	Submediant	Leading-tone
TYPE:	Major	Minor	Minor	Major	Major	Minor	Diminished

E minor (harmonic form).

FUNCTION:	Tonic	Supertonic	Mediant	Subdominant	Dominant	Submediant	Leading-tone
TYPE:	Minor	Diminished	Augmented	Minor	Major	Major	Diminished

Project 3

Major and Minor Triads in Root Position

Texture. The following exercises are to be played in four-part, chordal texture with all parts sounding simultaneously. Score order should be maintained, i.e., the soprano will sound above the alto, alto above tenor, and tenor above (or in unison with) bass. Each of the four parts should be scored within a practical vocal compass.[1]

Doubling. Each triad should have two roots, one third, and one fifth. In these first projects the root of the triad is always in the bass; each of the three upper parts will sound a different chord member.

Spacing. There are two possibilities.

1. Close structure. The soprano, alto, and tenor parts are assigned adjacent chord members. There is less than an octave between soprano and tenor parts. The three upper parts may be played with the right hand. Close structure chords may be notated with the tenor part in either treble or bass clef.

Bb major triad in close structure

2. Open structure. One chord member is omitted between soprano and alto and between alto and tenor. There is more than an octave between soprano and tenor. Play soprano and alto parts with the right hand, tenor and bass with the left.

E minor triad in open structure

[1]Since these exercises are intended for keyboard, rather than vocal performance, the range limitations may sometimes be relaxed at the discretion of the instructor.

It is easier for most people to play in close stucture, with three notes in the right hand. While it is acceptable to perform many of these exercises in close structure only, this practice will not always create the desired voice leading in all four parts. Open structure should be practiced now for increased application in later projects.

Figured bass. This notation system, initially developed as a practical musical shorthand, now serves primarily as an analytical and instructional tool. The symbols are Arabic numerals or accidentals written below the bass notes. They are to be interpreted as follows:

1. Numerals. These represent intervals above the bass note which are to be present in the chord; 6 indicates a sixth, 3 a third, etc.

2. Accidentals with numerals. Inflect (raise or lower chromatically) the tone which occurs at that interval above the bass.

3. Diagonal line through a numeral. The tone which occurs at the designated interval above the bass is to be chromatically raised.

4. Accidentals without numerals. These always refer to the tone which occurs a third above the bass.

Not all the notes to be played are prescribed by the figured bass; only the minimum figures necessary to a particular effect are employed. No symbols will appear to indicate the third or fifth of a root position triad unless a chomatic inflection is required.

The Arabic numerals indicate that certain notes are to be present, but they do not specify in which octave, or in which part, they should occur. Thus, the figured bass system symbolizes chord spelling, but not part-writing. A note or inflection designated by figures may occur in any of the upper parts, including the soprano.

I. Play the following triads as written and sing the chord members, 1-3-5-3-1, after you play. Identify the structure and the type (major or minor) of each triad.

II. Play the following triads in four parts with correct doubling and spacing. Analyze each as you play by identifying the function (chord name or number) in the key indicated. Note that capital letters denote major keys and lower-case letters denote minor keys. Use these exercises also to develop your ability to discriminate aurally between major and minor triads. Practice by playing the bass note and then singing either the entire triad (1-3-5-3-1) or the soprano note. Try to anticipate the sound of each chord before playing.

A. Close structure.

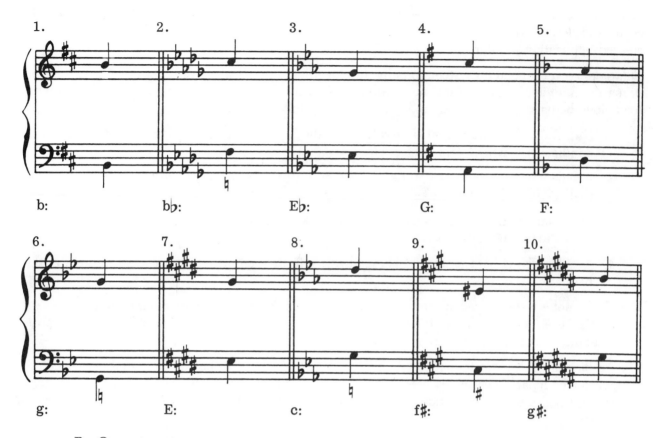

B. Open structure.

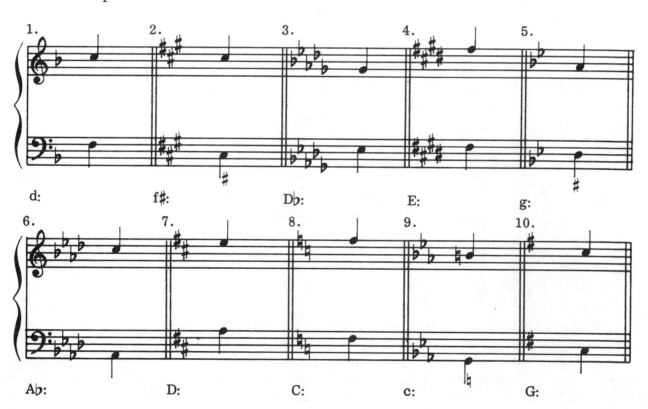

Repeated Triads

The relationship between two consecutive triads may be measured by the intervallic distance between the chord roots. Four such relationships are possible: (1) repeated triads (same root), (2) roots a fifth (or fourth) apart, (3) roots a second (or seventh) apart, and (4) roots a third (or sixth) apart. Analyze the root movements in the following example.

Ex. 4.1.   Stettin (Nun seht)

Many famous musical themes are constructed on a single triad. Two of these, both based on major triads, are shown below.

Ex. 4.2.   Beethoven, Symphony No. 3, Op. 55

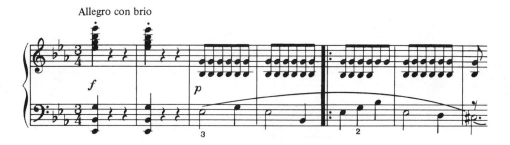

Ex. 4.3.   J. S. Bach, Violin Concerto in E Major

One of the basic principles of part-writing is that each part should retain its own melodic coherence and continuity. The most important means of achieving this is to move the parts as smoothly as possible and to avoid unnecessary or awkward melodic leaps.

In connecting repeated triads, two procedures are possible: (1) score both triads in the same (close or open) structure, or (2) change structure. In many situations either procedure will result in satisfactory voice-leading, and the choice between using close or open structure may be made solely on the basis of the type of vertical sonority desired. Retaining structure is always an acceptable procedure unless it results in excessive vocal ranges, or the soprano melody moves between non-adjacent chord tones. If a change of structure occurs, the higher of the two soprano notes must be harmonized in open structure.

Examine the scoring of repeated triads in these excerpts from church hymns, noting whether the structure is retained or changed.

Ex. 4.4.   Four hymn phrases.

Evan

Evening Praise

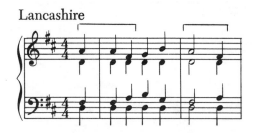

Lancashire

Regent Square

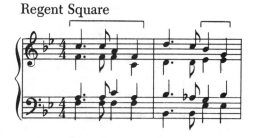

I. Retain structure.

In these connections no part will skip farther than a perfect fourth. Nos. 6-10 may be played in either open or close structure.

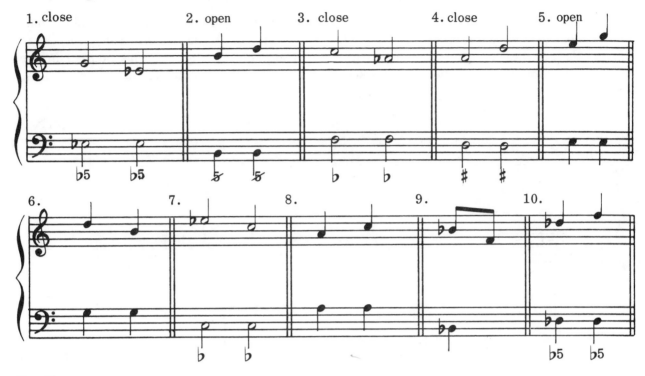

II. Change structure.

The higher soprano tone will be harmonized in open structure. These connections will always include a "common tone" (note repeated in the same part) in one of the inner voices.
These practices are illustrated in nos. 1 and 2.

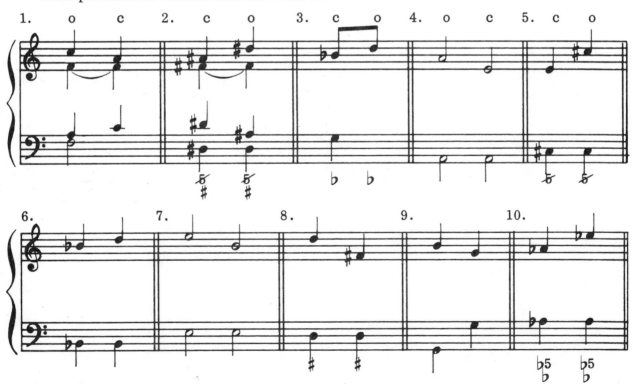

III. Chord tone melodies.

These melodies may be performed in two ways.

1. Play and sustain a tonic triad while singing the melody with scale degrees.

2. Harmonize in four parts, using the tonic triad throughout each melody. Remember that a change of structure is mandatory (only) when the soprano skips more than a fourth, and that, in these situations, the higher of the two soprano tones must be harmonized in open structure. These situations are marked by brackets, with the necessary structures indicated.

Roots a Fifth Apart—Tonic and Dominant

This category of relationships includes progressions in which the chord roots move up or down a fifth or a fourth. Root movements in fifths is the most definitive characteristic of tonal harmony. The following example illustrates how all the triads in a key are often arranged in a fifth related sequence: i - iv, VII - III, VI - ii°, V - i (mm. 6-13).

Ex. 5.1.   Tchaikovsky, Symphony No. 4, Op. 36

I. Cadences.

A cadence is a point of punctuation or of relative repose in the musical form. The identities of musical phrases and cadences are interdependent. A cadence forms the conclusion of a phrase, generally the last two chords. Cadences are classified according to their harmonic and melodic characteristics. Practice these cadences systematically in all major and minor keys.

Both triads should be scored in the same structure. As a result, none of the three upper parts will leap more than a third. Maintain normal doubling and spacing in all chords.   KEYS OF
C, G, D, A, F, B♭, E♭

A. Perfect-authentic cadence: $\dfrac{7 - 8}{\text{V} \quad \text{I}}$

B. Imperfect-authentic cadence: $\dfrac{5 - 3}{\text{V} \quad \text{I}}$

C. Half cadence (I to V): $\dfrac{1 - 2}{\text{I} \quad \text{V}}$ $\dfrac{3 - 2}{\text{I} \quad \text{V}}$ $\dfrac{8 - 7}{\text{I} \quad \text{V}}$

In these abstract settings, Arabic numerals represent soprano scale degrees (melody) and Roman numerals represent chords (harmony). Illustrations:

G: V   I   c: V   i   A♭:   V   I   d: V   i   B♭:   I   V   b: i   V   a: i   V

These progressions may be performed in either open or close structure. The student with limited piano facility may choose to do these only in close structure, playing the three triad tones with the right hand and the root with the left.

One practice technique is to combine all the progressions into one continuous phrase. Keep in mind, however, that a chord succession is not considered a cadence unless it occurs at the end of a phrase.

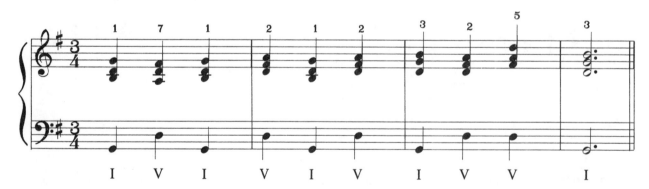

I   V   I   V   I   V   I   V   V   I

Proceed systematically through the twelve possible tonic centers, playing the major and minor key versions on each level, for instance: B♭, b♭, B, b, C, c, etc.

II. Sequences.

A musical sequence is a pattern which recurs successively on different pitch levels. It is an important organizing technique in tonal music, and can also be employed as an effective learning tool.

The tones of major and minor scales can be arranged in a series of fifths. In each series there will be five or six perfect fifths and one or two diminished fifths. In major keys, a diminished fifth occurs between the 4th and 7th scale degrees. In minor, the location of the diminished fifth varies according to the scale form used—between 4 and 7, 6 and 2, or both.

Similarly, each major or minor key will include one or two diminished triads—vii° in major and vii° and/or ii° in minor. The diminished triad sounds unstable in root position and so usually occurs in first inversion. Its use in root position is limited to sequential passages where the momentum of the reiterated pattern compensates for the inherent weakness of the diminished triad.

The sequences illustrated below use the white keys of the piano. They may be transposed to any key. In minor, the key center is more strongly established by chromatically raising the leading-tone, that is, by using the harmonic form of the scale. Play these sequences in several keys.

A. C major

B. A minor

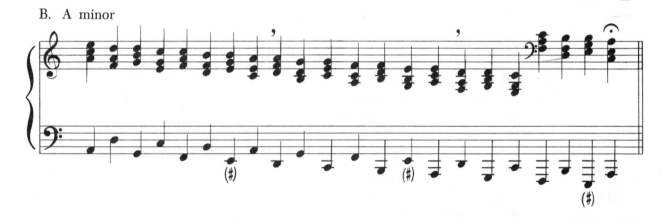

III. Triads with roots a fifth apart.

A. Various fifth relationships.

The techniques of part-writing are the same regardless of the harmonic function of the chords. Remember to play both chords in the same structure.

Learn to recognize the aural effect of root movement in fifths. Practice by playing the first chord, or bass tone, and then singing the root of the second chord before playing.

B. Phrases using tonic and dominant triads. A definite key center can be generated by using only these two triads. Analyze the cadences and classify each according to type.

As you practice these phrases, cultivate an awareness of the movement of the soprano melody within the key, as well as the harmonic progression. Sing the soprano and/or bass line with numbers.

IV. Melody harmonization using tonic and dominant triads in root position.

The harmonizing of a given soprano melody is accomplished by selecting a chord to accompany each melodic note. In this project chord choices are limited to two possibilities, tonic and dominant. The harmonic repertoire will be progressively expanded throughout the subsequent projects.

In approaching this problem systematically, the first step is to identify the key and scale degree numbers of the given melody. Secondly, select the chords which contain the melodic tones. Scale degrees may be accompanied by tonic or dominant triads as shown below.

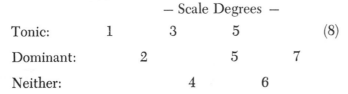

— Scale Degrees —

Tonic:	1	3	5	(8)
Dominant:	2		5	7
Neither:			4	6

Both triads contain the 5th scale degree. Scale degrees 4 and 6 cannot be harmonized with either of the two available chords.

Following are two sets of problems of increasing difficulty. Complete all phrases by harmonizing melodies in four parts.

A.

At this point in the study the 5th scale degree is the only one that offers a choice of harmonizing chords. In this situation chord selection is based on the requirements of harmonic rhythm or voice leading.

> *Harmonic rhythm.* Change chords on every strong beat. When the melody begins on a strong beat harmonize the first note with a tonic chord.

> *Voice leading.* Leaps in the soprano must be harmonized with repeated triads.

B.

Project 6

Roots a Fifth Apart—The Primary Triads

With the addition of the subdominant triad, the harmonic vocabulary now includes the three primary triads—the tonic, and the triads with roots a fifth above (dominant) and a fifth below (subdominant).

Ex. 6.1.   Wagner, Valhalla motive from "Das Rheingold"

Ex. 6.2.   Franck, Symphony in D Minor

I. The plagal cadence.

This cadence, consisting of the harmonic movement IV to I, often occurs as an extension of the phrase, following an authentic cadence. It is idiomatic as an "Amen" at the conclusion of church hymns.

Ex. 6.3.   Old Hundredth

The part-writing technique is the same as in Project 5; in fifth relationships, score both chords in the same structure, double the root in all chords.

Plagal cadence: $\dfrac{8-8}{IV\quad I}$ $\dfrac{4-3}{IV\quad I}$

Illustrations:

II. Phrases using the primary triads.

Play these phrases in four parts; analyze chords and cadences. Compare the aural effect of roots descending a fifth (V to I or I to IV) with that of roots ascending a fifth (I to V or IV to I). Sing the bass line with scale degree numbers before playing.

6.

7.

III. Melody harmonization.

A.

1. G major

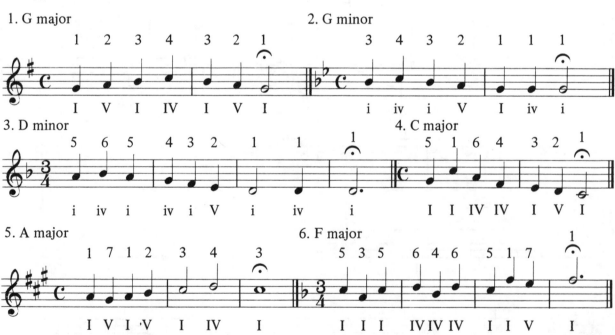

I V I IV I V I

2. G minor

i iv i V I iv i

3. D minor

i iv i iv i V i iv i

4. C major

I I IV IV I V I

5. A major

I V I V I IV I

6. F major

I I I IV IV IV I I V I

B.

The primary triads may be used in melody harmonization as follows:

—Scale Degrees—

Subdominant:	1		4	6	(8)
Tonic:	1	3	5		(8)
Dominant:		2	5	7	

These phrases should be harmonized using only chord repetition or root movement of a fifth. Remember that leaps larger than a third in the soprano must be accommodated by chord repetition. Sing or play through each melody before harmonizing.

Project 7

Roots a Second Apart

To connect two triads whose roots are at the interval of a second, move the three upper parts in contrary motion (i.e. opposite direction) to the bass to the nearest tones of the next chord. Thus, if the bass moves up a second, the three upper parts will descend. As with fifth relationships, both triads will be in the same structure. Continue to score all triads in root position and with the root doubled.

I. Additional half cadences and a typical progression of primary triads.

AVOID Par 5's + Par 8's by contrary motion in Bass v. Soprano

Risk of PAR 5's + 8's in IV–V Progression

      A. Half cadence:

$$\frac{8-7}{\text{IV} \quad \text{V}} \qquad \frac{6-5}{\text{IV} \quad \text{V}} \qquad \frac{4-2}{\text{IV} \quad \text{V}}$$

      B. Progression:

$$\frac{8-8-7-8}{\text{I} \quad \text{IV} \quad \text{V} \quad \text{I}} \qquad \frac{3-4-2-3}{\text{I} \quad \text{IV} \quad \text{V} \quad \text{I}}$$

Illustrations:

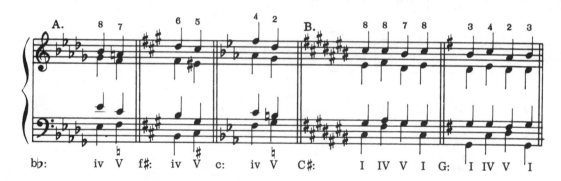

II. Sequences using root movement in fifths and seconds. Play these in several keys.

      A. Major keys.

B. Minor keys.

III. Phrases with figured bass. Various second relationships.

A. Analyze the chord functions as you play. Note the difference in the aural effect of ascending vs. descending second relationships.

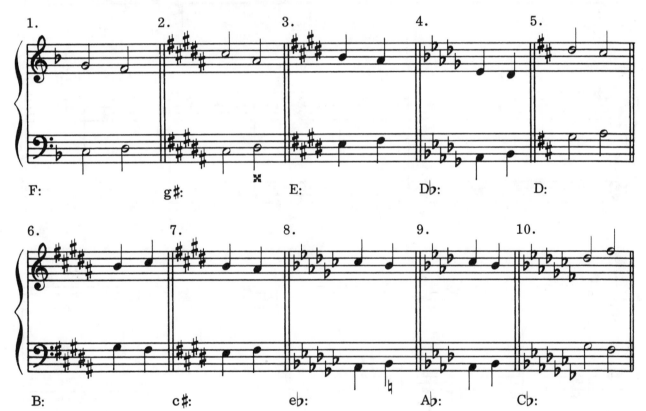

B. Phrases using tonic, dominant, and subdominant triads.

In the first four phrases direct applications of the typical I — IV — V — I progression are shown. Numerous other harmonic-melodic combinations are also illustrated. Note the rather striking effect of the progression V — IV.

IV. Melody harmonization using the primary triads in root position.

Use chord repetition or root movement of a fifth or a second. Keep these points in mind: (1) repeat the chord when the soprano skips more than a third, (2) changes of structure may occur only in chord repetition, and (3) change the chord at each accented beat.

A typical harmonic progression of primary triads moves from subdominant to dominant (ascending second) and from dominant to tonic (descending fifth).

The tonic chord regularly moves to either IV or V (ascending or descending fifths).

The progression V — IV (descending second) is in opposition to the normal flow of harmony toward the tonic and is of much less frequent occurrence.

These melodies include some direct applications of the harmonic progression I-IV-V-I studied earlier in this project.

A.

1. G major   2. B minor

First Inversion of Triads

A triad is said to be in first inversion when the third of the chord is in the bass. The potential for inversion adds a significant dimension to an otherwise simple triad vocabulary. These sonorities are distinctive and readily distinguishable from root-position chords. The unique sound of first-inversion triads is an important feature of the theme of the final movement of Brahms' Fourth Symphony.

Ex. 8.1.   Brahms, Fourth Symphony

A second advantage offered by the use of inversions is the possibility for increased melodic interest in the bass line. Observe how stepwise motion in the bass is achieved by the judicious use of first inversions. The varied re-harmonization of the same chorale phrase, with chromaticism added, should also be noted.

Ex. 8.2.   Bach, Chorale 142, phrases 1 and 3

First inversion is indicated by the figured bass numerals 6 or ⁶₃. Generally the best vertical effect, and the smoothest voice-leading, is achieved when the note which appears in the *soprano* part—whether it is the root, third, or fifth of the triad—is doubled.

When triads are inverted an additional structural possibility is created. Inverted triads commonly occur with the soprano and tenor parts exactly an octave apart. The term "neutral structure" may be used to describe these sonorities.

Thus, triads in first inversion can be scored in close, open, or neutral structure. These spacings are defined by the distance between tenor and soprano voices:

1. close structure, less than an octave.

2. open structure, more than an octave.

3. neutral structure (first inversion only), tenor and soprano doubled at the octave.

Compare the structures of root position and inverted triads.

I. Triads in first inversion.

Play and analyze these first-inversion triads; double the soprano in each. Functional analysis and chord spelling is based on the chord root in inversions as well as in root position triads. Isolate and sing chord roots as you play.

A. Close structure.   B. Open structure.

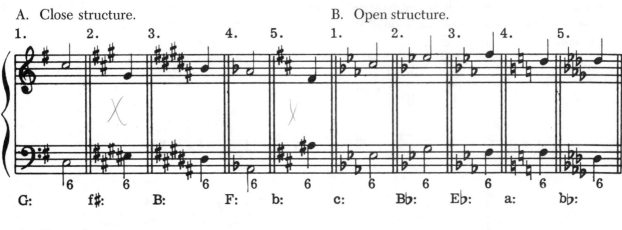

C. Neutral structure.

Independence of Parts

In Project 3 one of the fundamental principles of part-writing was presented, namely, that each of the parts should maintain its own melodic coherence and continuity. With basic harmonic materials this is achieved simply by moving each part the smallest possible distance as it weaves through the musical texture, and by avoiding awkward melodic intervals. A second principle, equally vital, is that each part should maintain a maximum degree of melodic independence from all other parts .

The relationship between the melodic movement of any two parts may be classified as follows.

Contrary motion: parts move in opposite directions.

Oblique motion: one part is stationary or repeated.

Similar motion: parts move varying distances in the same direction.

Parallel motion: parts move the same distance in the same direction.

Contrary and oblique motion serve best to differentiate parts. In similar or parallel motion the identity of the two parts tends to merge and the integrity of each part is somewhat diminished.

Two parts which sound at the most-consonant intervals of the perfect octave or perfect fifth also momentarily sacrifice some degree of their independence. It is desirable then that their individuality be re-asserted by proceeding from these vertical intervals by contrary or oblique motion. The techniques previously considered for connecting root-position triads have served to accomplish this, as may be observed in the following example.

Movement from octaves: Movement from fifths:

In fifth relationships between root-position triads, octaves and fifths are sometimes left by similar motion. The direction of the bass line is usually the determining factor in these situations, as may be seen in the following examples. Notice also that overlapping of parts occasionally occurs between bass and tenor, as in no. 3a. These conditions should usually be avoided in progressing from inverted triads.

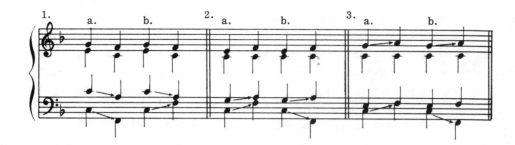

II. Additional cadences.

Play these cadences in all major and minor keys. Double the soprano in each inverted chord and move from this doubled tone in contrary or oblique motion.

A. Authentic cadence: $\dfrac{5-3}{V^6 \quad I}$ $\dfrac{2-3}{V^6 \quad I}$ $\dfrac{2-1}{V^6 \quad I}$

B. Half cadences: $\dfrac{8-7}{I^6 \quad V}$ $\dfrac{3-2}{I^6 \quad V}$

$\dfrac{4-5}{IV^6 \quad V}$ $\dfrac{4-2}{IV^6 \quad V}$

Illustrations:

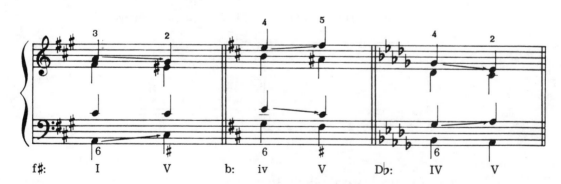

An inverted chord in neutral structure may, under various conditions, progress to a root-position chord in either close or open structure. Consequently, the use of inversion may provide a means for changing structure without repeating a chord. Observe the smooth voice-leading in these examples.

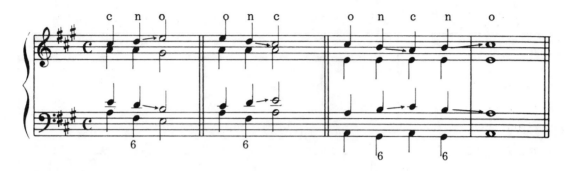

III. Sequences using triads in root position and first inversion. Play in various major and minor keys. In minor, raise the leading tone only at the end of the passage.

A.

B.   C.

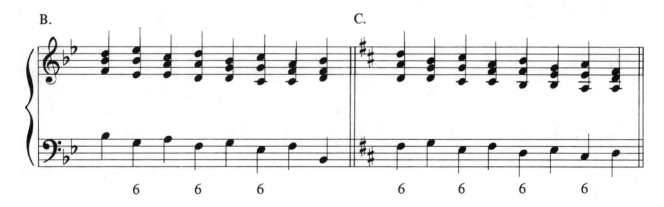

IV. Phrases using primary triads in root position and first inversion.

Play and analyze; indications of structure are included in the first four phrases. Listen carefully
to the harmonic progression; practice singing the chord roots as you play.

10.

Successive Inverted Triads

We have seen that doubling the soprano tone in first-inversion triads usually produces the best result. When two or more inverted triads are used in direct succession, however, it is often necessary to alternate the doublings in order to retain the melodic independence of each part. Either the bass note, or the inner parts, may be doubled in these situations, with the limitation that the most active tones, the leading-tone as well as the raised sixth degree in melodic minor, should not be doubled.

Within the present chord vocabulary, the most difficult problem arises in progressing from subdominant to dominant when both triads are in first inversion. The problem is particularly acute in minor keys, since the bass (raised sixth or seventh) should not be doubled in either chord. Some solutions are shown below in E major. The first two harmonizations of each soprano line are appropriate also to minor keys. Note that the movement from the doubled tone is always in contrary motion.

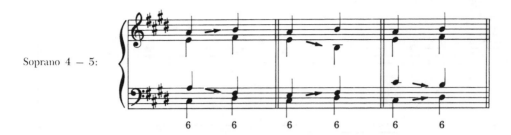

Soprano 4 — 5:

V. Phrases with figured bass, including consecutive inversions.

Some possible solutions for these difficult situations are indicated.

Sing the chord roots, either with "la" or with the scale degree numbers 1, 4, or 5. This exercise is particularly beneficial if you can sing the next chord root *before* actually playing the chord.

VI. Melody harmonization using primary triads in root position and first inversion.

Leaps of a fourth in the soprano may now be harmonized either by chord repetition or by chord change with one of the two chords scored in first inversion. The choice will be determined by the requirements of the harmonic rhythm.

The use of inversions adds greater variety to the vertical sonorities and enhances the potential for increased step-wise motion in the bass line. Plan your harmonizations carefully. Determine the chords and develop a good bass line, using appropriate inversions, before you add the inner parts. Sing the bass part as you play.

A.

1. G minor

2. F major

3. E minor

4. Ab major

5. D minor

6. G major

B.

1.   2.   3.

4.   5.

6.

Project 9

Second Inversion of the Tonic Triad

Second inversion, with the chord fifth in the bass, is designated by the numerals $^6_4$ in the figured bass. The use of second inversion is restricted to a very few carefully controlled situations, the most common of these being the tonic triad in second inversion preceding the perfect-authentic cadence.

Other applications of second inversion—as passing, pedal, and arpeggiated six-four chords—are to be presented later, in Project 15.

Examine the uses of the cadential tonic six-four chord in the following hymn phrases.

Ex. 9.1.   Four hymn phrases.

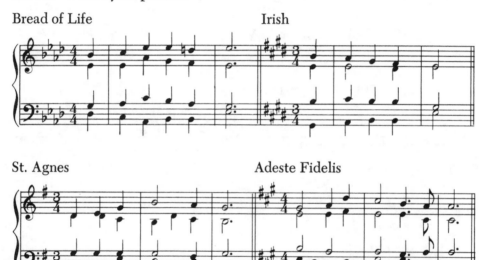

The following procedures may be observed:

1. The bass of the six-four chord is approached by step, and is doubled.

2. The six-four chord occurs on an accented beat, or on the second beat of a three-beat measure.

3. The intervals of a sixth and a fourth above the bass move down by step to a fifth and third, forming a dominant chord.

I. Typical settings.

Learn in all keys. In these progressions the first and third chords, I and I^6_4, are scored exactly alike except for the bass.

$$\frac{8-8-8-7-8}{\text{I \quad IV \quad I}^6_4 \text{ \quad V \quad I}} \qquad \frac{3-4-3-2-1}{\text{I \quad IV \quad I}^6_4 \text{ \quad V \quad I}}$$

44

Illustrations:

II. Phrases.

Play and analyze, noting especially the effect of the cadential tonic six-four. The tonic function of this chord is obscured by the emphasis placed on the fifth scale degree.

5.

STEPWISE CONTRARY MOTION

6.   7.

III. Melody harmonization using the cadential tonic six-four.

A.

1. C minor

2. G major

3. D minor

4. E♭ major

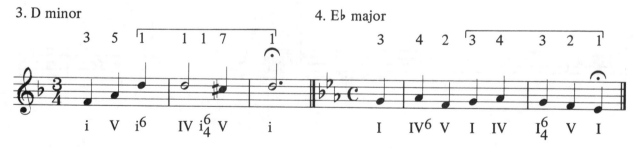

B.

Project 10

The Leading-Tone Triad

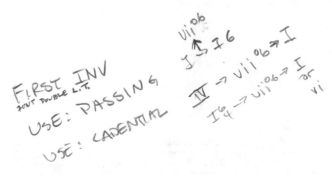

The triads built on the leading-tone in major and minor keys and on the supertonic in minor are classified as diminished, having the intervals of a diminished fifth and a minor third above the root. They are relatively unstable vertical sonorities and are most effective in first inversion.

The leading-tone triad may be considered a contrapuntal chord since it is usually resolved with smooth voice leading in all parts. It includes the active scale degrees 2, 4, and 7 which resolve by step to a tonic triad.

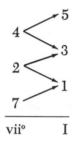

This chord is often used to connect root position and first inversion of the tonic triad. A second idiomatic use is between IV and I or I^6.

$$I \rightarrow vii^{o6} \rightarrow I$$
$$IV \rightarrow vii^{o6} \rightarrow I^6$$

Observe the use of vii^{o6} in the following examples.

Ex. 10.1. Schumann, Chorale from Album for the Young

Ex. 10.2. Telemann, St. Luke Passion

48

I. An additional cadence; typical settings.

As with other first inversions, it is customary to double the tone which appears in the soprano part. If the leading tone is in the soprano, however, it is necessary to double the bass.

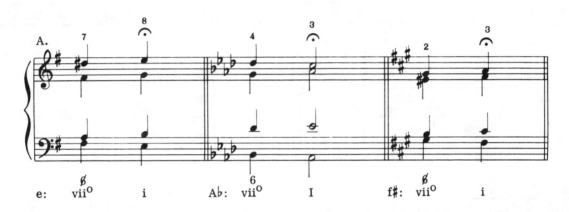

A. Imperfect-authentic cadence:

$$\frac{7-8}{vii^{o6} \quad I} \qquad \frac{4-3}{vii^{o6} \quad I} \qquad \frac{2-3}{vii^{o6} \quad I}$$

B.

$$\frac{3-4-3-4-3}{I \quad vii^{o6} \quad I^6 \quad vii^{o6} \quad I} \qquad \frac{3-2-1-2-3}{I \quad vii^{o6} \quad I^6 \quad vii^{o6} \quad I} \qquad \frac{1-7-1-7-1}{I \quad vii^{o6} \quad I^6 \quad vii^{o6} \quad I}$$

C.

$$\frac{5-6-7-8}{I \quad IV \quad vii^{o6} \quad I} \qquad \frac{3-4-4-3}{I \quad IV \quad vii^{o6} \quad I} \qquad \frac{1-1-2-3}{I \quad IV \quad vii^{o6} \quad I}$$

Illustrations:

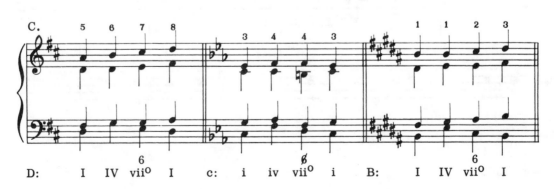

II. The diminished triad.

This sonority is aurally distinguished from major and minor triads by its lack of a perfect fifth. The root of a diminished triad is consequently more obscure and more difficult to extract.

1. Compare the sound of perfect and diminished fifths. Sing perfect fifths, "one-five," followed by diminished fifths on the same root.

2. Sing diminished triads using a given tone as root, third, or fifth: 1-3-5-3-1, 3-1-3-5-3-1, and 5-1-3-5-3-1.

III. Phrases with figured bass.

Sing the diminished triads as they appear.

✱ LEADING TONE in SOP ⟹ OPEN or CLOSE, NOT N or HN ✱

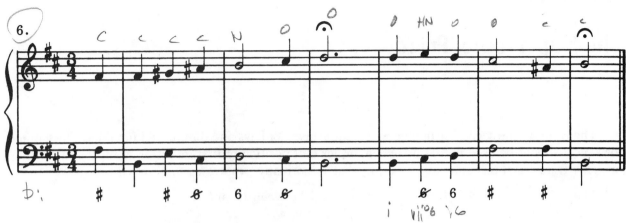

IV. Melody harmonization.

Use at least one leading-tone triad in each—to harmonize scale degrees 7, 2, or 4. The progression IV — vii°⁶ — I is the most effective way to harmonize 6 — 7 — 8 in the soprano melody.

A.

1. B minor

2. A♭ major

3. C minor

4. D♭ major

B.

1.

2.

3.

4.

5.

6.

Project 11

The Supertonic Triad

TONIC SUPERTONIC INV
MAJOR MINOR ROOT, FIRST
MINOR DIMINISHED) FIRST

DBL
ROOT / THIRD

The triad on the second scale degree is minor in major keys and diminished in minor. Thus, in minor keys it should be used in first inversion; either root position or first inversion is appropriate in major. This triad functions similarly to IV in that it normally progresses to V or vii°⁶.

The tonic six-four chord may be interpolated between ii⁶ and V.

Double either the root or the third of the chord, whichever will produce the smoother voice-leading.

An alternative procedure for connecting two root position triads with roots a second apart is to double the third in the second chord. This may be necessary, for instance, in the progression I—ii in order to avoid excessive parallel motion.

Several applications of the supertonic triad are illustrated below.

Ex. 11.1. Four phrases from chorale harmonizations.

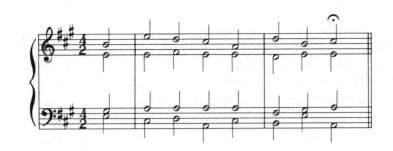

I.   Additional half-cadences and two typical settings.

A.   Half cadences.

$$\frac{4 - 2}{ii \quad V}$$
or
ii^6

$$\frac{2 - 7}{ii \quad V}$$
or
ii^6

B.   Compare with IB in Project 7.

$$\frac{3 - 4 - 2 - 3}{I \quad ii \quad V \quad I}$$
or
ii^6

$$\frac{3 - 2 - 2 - 1}{I \quad ii \quad V \quad I}$$
or
ii^6

C.   Compare with I in Project 9.

$$\frac{3 - 4 - 3 - 2 - 1}{I \quad ii^6 \quad I^6_4 \quad V \quad I}$$

$$\frac{3 - 2 - 1 - 7 - 1}{I \quad ii^6 \quad I^6_4 \quad V \quad I}$$

Illustrations:

Note that in minor keys, the supertonic triad is used only in first inversion. A subtle point of part-writing is illustrated in letter B below. In the illustration in B-flat minor the interval of a fifth between alto and tenor in the first chord is left in parallel motion. Careful scrutiny, however, will reveal that the interval between these parts in the second chord is a diminished, rather than perfect, fifth. This dissonance serves to retain the independence of the parts. In major keys this progression must be done in close structure.

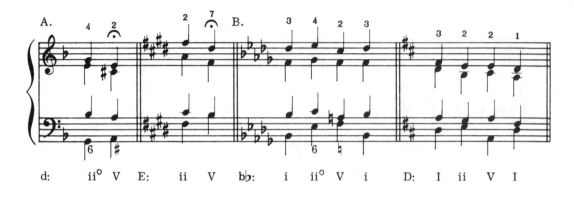

d: ii°   V   E: ii   V   bb: i   ii°   V   i   D: I   ii   V   I

f#:   i   ii°   i   V   i   Bb: I   ii   I   V   I

II. Sequence.

This pattern should be played in various major and minor keys. Use close structure only, as illustrated.

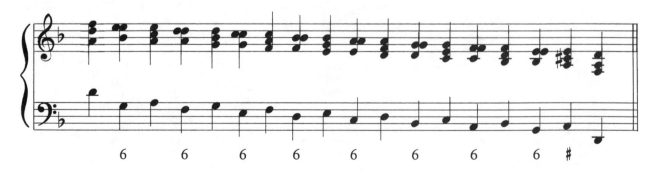

III. Phrases with figured bass.

Observe the very strong tonal effect of the progression ii − V − I, characterized by root movement in descending fifth. The triads ii and vii°⁶ have two tones in common; the progression may be accomplished by moving only one part by step. This procedure is included in phrases 3 and 5.

IV. Melody harmonization.

The supertonic triad is most often used to harmonize the second or fourth scale degrees. Sing the chord roots as you play.

A.

B.

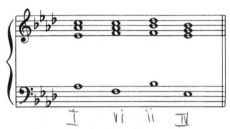

The Submediant Triad—Roots a Third Apart

The submediant triad is minor in major keys, major in minor, and appears most commonly in root position. This chord shares two tones, scale degrees one and three, with the tonic triad and may be used as an optional substitute for that chord in two general contexts.

The vi may be inserted after I in the progressions I→ii(^{6}) or I→IV to add variety or color in a harmonization. When it precedes ii, vi extends the basic tonal progression of root movement in descending fifths.

A unique effect occurs when the submediant triad follows the dominant. This is especially notable when it is used at the end of a phrase and is aptly referred to as a deceptive cadence. Observe the use of the submediant triad in the following examples.

Ex. 12.1. Four phrases from chorale harmonizations.

Ex. 12.2. Wagner, Grail Motive from Parsifal

I. Deceptive cadence and typical settings.

In the progression V—vi, use the alternative part-writing for roots a second apart, i.e., double the third in the submediant triad. Note that B and C simply add vi to typical settings from Projects 7 and 11.

A. Deceptive cadence:

$$\frac{7-8}{\text{V} \quad \text{vi}} \qquad \frac{2-1}{\text{V} \quad \text{vi}}$$

B.

$$\frac{1-1-2-7-1}{\text{I} \quad \text{vi} \quad \text{ii} \quad \text{V} \quad \text{I}} \qquad \frac{3-3-4-2-3}{\text{I} \quad \text{vi} \quad \text{ii} \quad \text{V} \quad \text{1}}$$

or
ii⁶

or
ii⁶

C.

$$\frac{3-3-4-2-3}{\text{I} \quad \text{vi} \quad \text{IV·} \quad \text{V} \quad \text{I}} \qquad \frac{1-1-1-7-1}{\text{I} \quad \text{vi} \quad \text{IV} \quad \text{V} \quad \text{I}}$$

Illustrations

C.

Db: I   vi   IV   V   I   c#:   i   VI   iv   V   i

II. Sequences.

A.

I   vi   IV   ii   VII°   V   I

B.

III. Various third relationships.

A. Play and analyze, observing carefully the aural effect of these root relationships.

Eb: I   vi♭   f#:   Gb: b: F:

D: bb: E: f: c#:

B. Phrases.

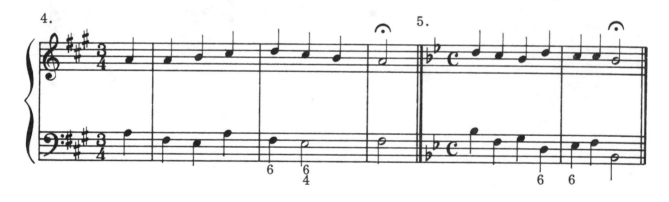

f: V i VI iv V i   f#: I vi   V VI

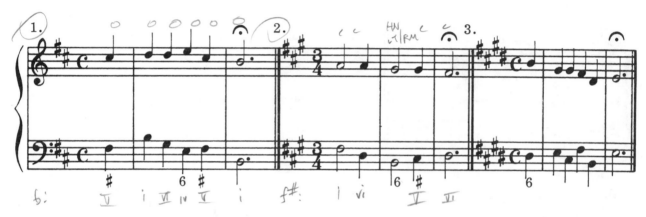

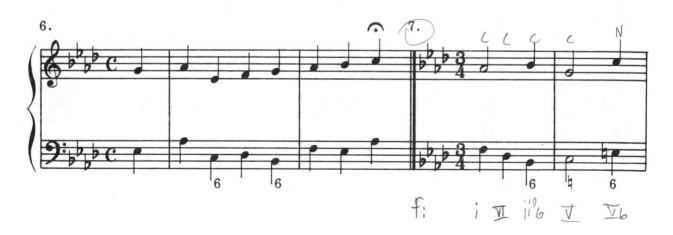

f: i VI ii°6 V VI6

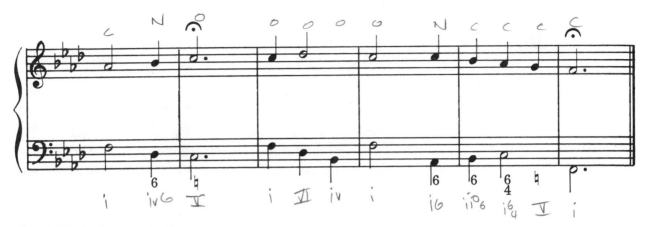

IV. Melody harmonization.

The submediant triad commonly harmonizes the first or third scale degrees.

Project 13

The Mediant Triad

The addition of this chord completes the harmonic vocabulary of diatonic triads. The mediant triad is minor in major keys and major or augmented in minor. In its basic tonal context, this chord precedes vi in a series of descending fifth relationships, iii — vi — ii — V — I, as in this famous passage.

Ex. 13.1.   Wagner, "Wedding March" from *Lohengrin*

There are, in addition, two special uses of the mediant triad. The first of these is in harmonizing the melodic passage 8 — 7 — 6 in which the leading-tone (or subtonic in minor) descends. The progression, I or vi — iii — IV, is used in this situation.

Ex. 13.2.   Ein' feste Burg

The mediant triad has two tones in common with V and with I⁶₄. It may appear in first inversion in connection with (or in lieu of) either of these chords. In minor the seventh scale degree will be raised, creating an augmented mediant triad. The bass is usually doubled. Note the similarities between III⁺⁶, i⁶₄, and V:

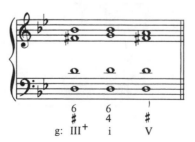

62

A common cadence design, based on this relationship, is illustrated below.

Ex. 13.3. Cadences from Bach chorale harmonizations

No. 200   No. 100

I. Typical settings.

A.

$$\frac{1 - 7 - 1 - 2 - 7 - 1}{\text{I} \quad \text{iii} \quad \text{vi} \quad \text{ii} \quad \text{V} \quad \text{I}} \qquad \frac{3 - 3 - 3 - 4 - 2 - 3}{\text{I} \quad \text{iii} \quad \text{vi} \quad \text{ii}^6 \quad \text{V} \quad \text{I}}$$

or
ii⁶

B.

$$\frac{8 - 7 - 6 - 5}{\text{I} \quad \text{iii} \quad \text{IV} \quad \text{I}}$$

C.   OPEN

$$\frac{3 - 4 - 3 - 2 - 1}{\text{I} \quad \text{ii}^6 \quad \text{iii}^6 \quad \text{V} \quad \text{I}}$$

Illustrations

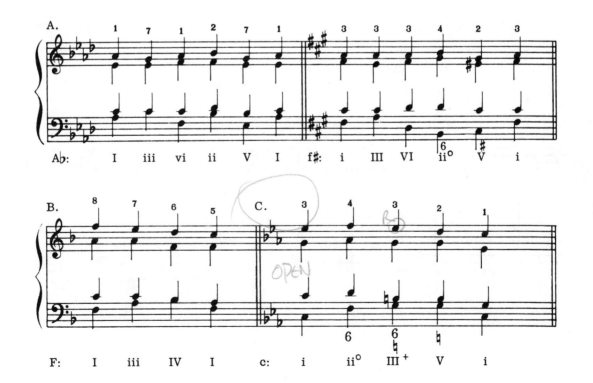

Keys Mm
C G D A E
F B♭ E♭

II. The augmented triad.

The augmented triad may impart a uniquely poignant color to a musical passage. It appears in the second measure of the operatic motive quoted below. The fourth measure of this example contains another colorful chord, the French sixth, which is examined in detail in Project 34.

Ex. 13.4. Puccini, Madame Butterfly, Act II

Copyright © 1954 by G. Ricordi & Co. Used by permission of Associated Music Publishers, Inc.

The distinctive color of this sonority relates to its symmetrical construction. It is comprised of superimposed major thirds and divides an octave into four equal parts. The identity of the chord root is ambiguous.

1. Aurally compare perfect and augmented fifths by singing both intervals from a given root tone.

2. Sing augmented triads using a given tone as root, third, or fifth.

III. Phrases with figured bass.

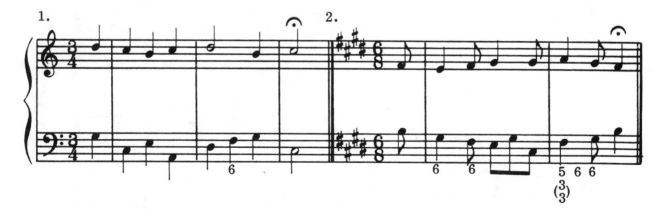

IV. Melody harmonization.

The mediant triad most often harmonizes the third scale degree $\left(\dfrac{3-3}{\text{iii} - \text{vi}}, \dfrac{3-2}{\text{iii}^6 - \text{V}}, \dfrac{3-4}{\text{iii}^6 - \text{IV}^6}\right)$ or the seventh scale degree $\left(\dfrac{7-8}{\text{iii} - \text{vi}}, \dfrac{7-6}{\text{iii} - \text{IV}}\right)$.

A.

1. C major

I   iii   vi   ii⁶   V   I

2. D major

I   iii   IV   I   ii⁶   I⁶₄   V   I

3. G minor   4. E minor

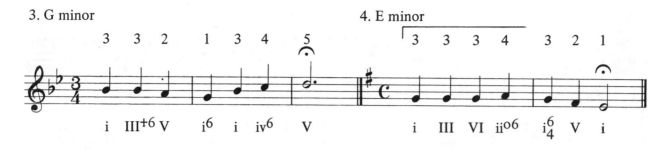

i III⁺⁶ V   i⁶ i iv⁶   V   i   III   VI   ii°⁶   i⁶₄ V   i

B.

Review: Melody Harmonization with Triads

In any major or minor key there are seven diatonic tones, each of which serves as the root of a triad. Tonal music is strongly characterized by the organization of these triads in descending fifth relationships.

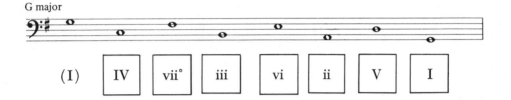

The triads on the subdominant and leading tone more commonly appear in later positions in this pattern, where they function as alternates to ii and V.

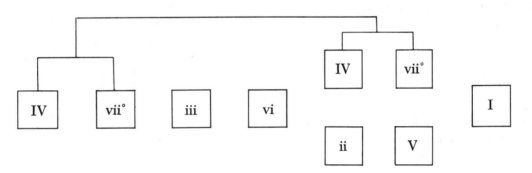

Root movement toward the tonic by fifths may take alternate paths.

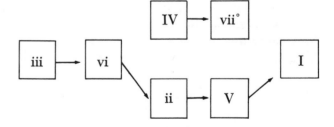

Other normal harmonic progressions are by ascending seconds—

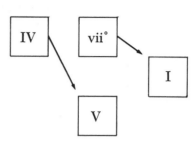

and descending thirds.

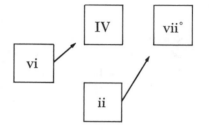

The combination of these three typical relationships—by descending fifths, ascending seconds, and descending thirds—illustrates normal harmonic progression.

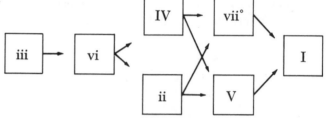

We have seen that other types of harmonic movement are also employed. These include harmonic repetition, elision, and retrogression.

Chord repetition, or movement between triads with similar functions, is not uncommon. Movement toward the tonic is momentarily retarded.

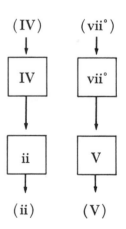

Movement toward the tonic may be accelerated by omitting a chord from a normal harmonic progression. This type of chord movement is termed harmonic elision.

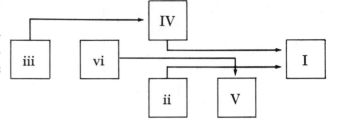

Harmonic retrogression, temporary movement away from the tonic, results in root relationships of descending or ascending seconds, or ascending fifths. This is the least common type of harmonic movement in tonal music.

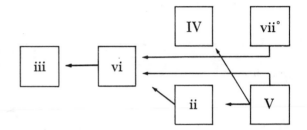

Processes in Melody Harmonization

1. Determine the key.
2. Select appropriate triads.
3. Refine the bass line.
4. Add inner parts.

1. *Determine the key.* The key signature is the primary indication. Remember that any key signature is applicable to a pair of relative keys, one major and one minor. Secondly, examine the cadences which conclude each phrase and select cadential chords. Most cadences are either authentic, ending with scale degrees 1 or 3 in the soprano, or half, ending with 2 or 7 in the soprano.

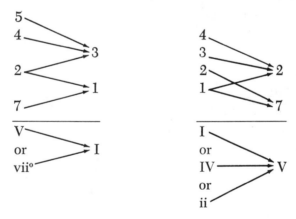

2. *Select appropriate triads.* The triads most closely related to the key center—I, V, IV, ii, vii°—occur most frequently. Harmonic variety will enhance the musical effect, but it is also useful to remember that most melodies could be harmonized using only the primary triads. Half notes in the soprano are most effectively harmonized by changing the chord, or the inversion, on the second beat.

3. *Refine the bass line.* The bass should be melodically complementary to the soprano. Typically, chorale bass lines move conjunctly (by step) except at cadences. Use *inversions* to create melodic interest. All major and minor triads may be used in root position and first inversion except the submediant, which is rarely inverted. Diminished and augmented triads occur in first inversion only. The cadential tonic six-four is the only common use of second inversion.

4. *Add inner parts.* The basic principles of part-writing have previously been summarized as: (a) melodic coherence of each part—move all parts as conjunctly as possible, and (b) independence of parts—move from vertical octaves and fifths in contrary or oblique motion.

These four processes are of course interrelated and interdependent. Spontaneous harmonization at the keyboard requires an agile mind and a keen musical intuition. Practice slowly at first, testing the effect with your ear as well as your intellect, but keep the tempo regular.

I. Chorale phrases with figured bass.

II. Additional chorale melodies for harmonization.

Unit II
Diatonic Modulation, Nonharmonic Tones, Seventh Chords

Project 15

Extensions of the Triad Vocabulary

I. Additional part-writing procedures.

The most common techniques for connecting triads have been presented in previous projects. Other procedures are occasionally encountered, of which two are perhaps the most important.

1. In connecting root-position triads with roots a fifth apart, a change of structure is possible. Hold the common tone and move one part the interval of a fourth.

2. The tonic triad may sometimes appear with three roots, one third, and no fifth.

Both of these procedures find their best use at the perfect-authentic cadence, although the first may sometimes harmonize the leap of a fourth in the soprano.

II. Further use of second inversion.

1. Passing six-four. The bass and soprano move stepwise in parallel or contrary motion.

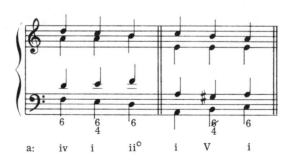

2. Pedal six-four. The bass is stationary; the six-four chord is preceded and followed by the same root-position triad.

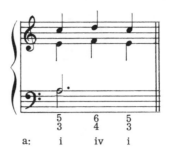

3. Arpeggiated six-four. The cadential tonic six-four is approached by a leap in the bass.

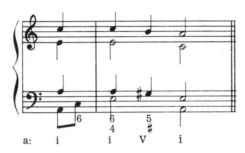

These settings of second inversions should be used sparingly, and only with primary triads.

Identify these alternative procedures in the hymn phrases below.

Ex. 15.1. Six hymn phrases

III. The subtonic in minor.

The use of the lowered seventh scale degree in a minor key may result in a major III (see Project 13), a major VII, or a minor v. Most commonly the lowered seventh will descend melodically to the lowered sixth — in the soprano (i — III — iv) or the bass (i — v⁶ — iv⁶). The subtonic triad may be used in connection with a chromatic bass, or preceding III in a fifth related sequence.

Observe the use of the subtonic in the following chorale phrases. Since the subtonic and mediant triads are far removed from the tonic, in terms of fifth relations, they strongly suggest modulation to the relative major key. The progression VII — III in minor sounds like V — I in the relative major.

Ex. 15.2. Five chorale phrases.

IV. Phrases with figured bass.

Play and analyze, noting the special harmonic effects described in this project.

8.

Diatonic Modulation (I)

Modulation is the process of moving from one key center to another. By means of modulation the tonal system is greatly expanded; harmonic relationships are extended to include not only chords, but entire key systems as well. There are several techniques by which a change of key may be accomplished. The present topic is diatonic modulation; chromatic and enharmonic modulations will be considered in subsequent projects.

These opening phrases from Bach chorale harmonizations illustrate the technique. Observe that these excerpts do not begin and end in the same key. Try to identify where the modulations occur.

Ex. 16.1. Bach, Four chorale phrases

Any triad may function in any of several capacities, depending on the prevailing key. C-major and A-minor triads, for example, might occur in any of the following contexts.

Diatonic modulation exploits this potential by using a chord which is common to two keys as a harmonic pivot to shift from one to the other. The procedure is aptly referred to as common chord modulation.

Modulation most frequently occurs within a family of near-related keys—those whose signatures are either the same, or different by only one accidental. Every key has five near-related keys which may be derived from the major and minor triads of that scale. The near-related keys to E major have signatures of four, or three or five, sharps.

The keys associated with E minor have one sharp, two, or none. The natural scale generates the near-related keys in minor.

Key relationships may also be classified according to the interval separating the two tonics—similar to root relationships between triads.

	Fifths		*Seconds*	*Thirds*	
E major:	B(V),	A(IV)	f♯(ii)	c♯(vi),	g♯(iii)
E minor:	b(v),	a(iv)	D(VII)	C(VI),	G(III)

I. Progressions using a given triad in two keys.

Improvise two complete resolutions for each of these triads in the keys indicated. Your progression should be based on the typical triad settings from previous projects, i.e., use normal harmonic progression and conclude each phrase with an authentic cadence. Identify aurally (play and sing) the tonic of each key before playing.

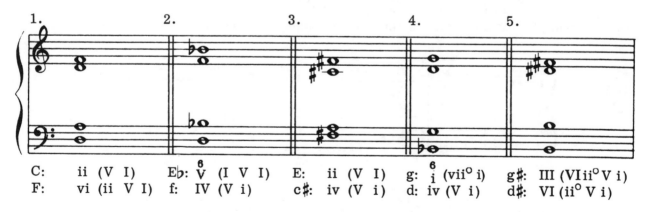

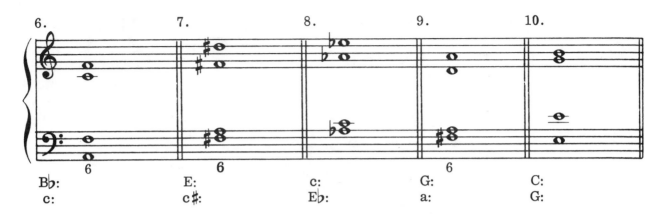

Diatonic modulation is achieved through three general steps:

1. Establish the original key.

2. Arrive at a common chord and exchange its function.

3. Establish the new key.

The leading-tone, the most active scale degree, plays a decisive role in establishing a key center. Project 4 demonstrated that a tonic orientation may be generated using only tonic and dominant triads. The leading-tone triad is only slightly less decisive than the dominant in this capacity.

II. Phrases with common chord modulations.

These phrases use the common chords from Exercise I. Identify the original tonic before playing. Then play the phrase, aurally compare the original and new key centers, and analyze the intervallic relationship between them. Analyze also the function of the common chord in both keys.

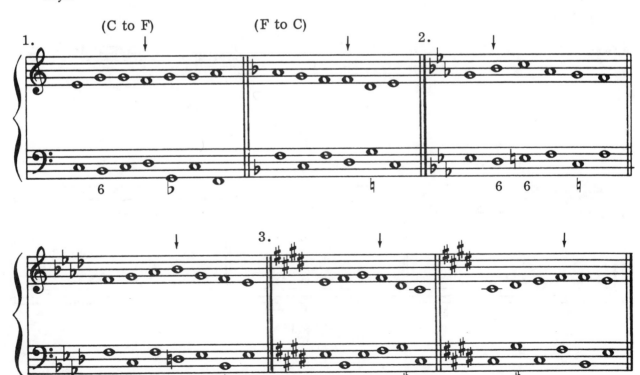

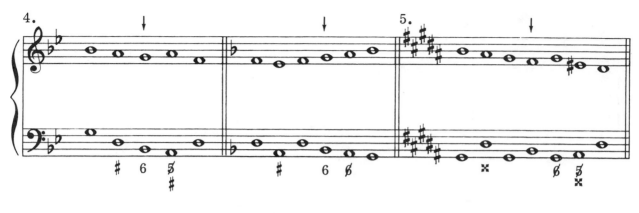

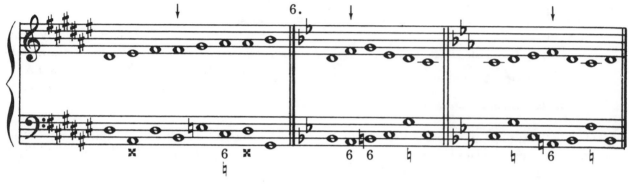

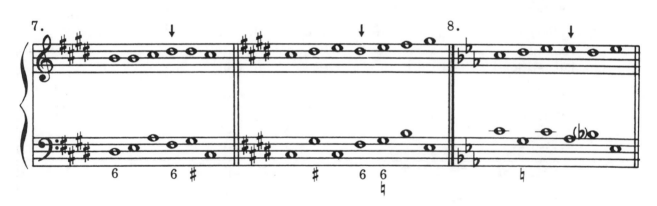

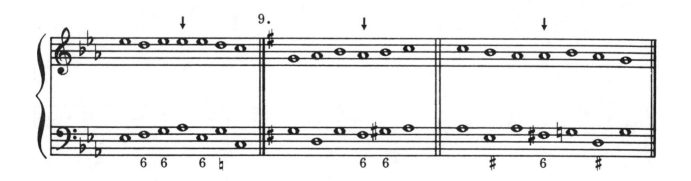

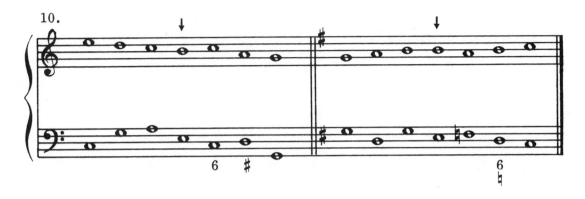

III. Modulations with chords specified.

Any pair of near-related keys will have several (two to five) triads in common which may function as pivots in a diatonic modulation. Some of the simplest and most direct modulations are abstracted below. Play these in various keys, concentrating on the aural relationship between the two tonic centers. Sing and remember the original tonic. Play the modulation, then sing and compare the original and new tonics.

The soprano melodies should move generally by step and in the lower tetrachord of the scales. The symbol ⌐ may be read as "becomes," e.g., "ii becomes vi." Inversions may be included as appropriate.

		From Major Keys	*From Minor Keys*
Fifth relationships: pivots ii-vi and i-iv.	To dominant key	I V I vi⌐ ⌐ii V I	i V i i⌐ ⌐iv V i
	To subdominant key	I V I ii⌐ ⌐vi ii V I	i V i iv⌐ ⌐i V i
Second relationships: pivots i-ii.	To supertonic key	I V I ii⌐ ⌐i V i	
	To subtonic key		i V i i⌐ ⌐ii V I
Third relationships: pivots i-vi.	To submediant key	I V I vi⌐ ⌐i V i	i V i VI⌐ ⌐I V I
	To mediant key	I V I⌐ ⌐VI ii° V i	i V i iv⌐ ⌐ii V I

Project 17

Diatonic Modulation (II)

A modulating phrase may contain several triads in succession which are common to both keys. Such an occurrence is especially probable when the two keys involved are major-minor relatives (having the same signatures). In the following harmonic situation there are four triads which could function in either key.

Triads (root & type):	C	G	C	a	F	d	b°	E	a

	C major:	I	V	I	vi	IV	ii	vii°		

Functions

	A minor:			i	VI	iv	ii°	V	i

While there are several common chords in this example, the modulation actually pivots on only one. The key of C major having been established, the ear will retain this key center until hearing the E major chord which has no diatonic function in C. Until this new dominant is sounded the phrase could proceed in either key. The chord immediately preceding is the essential pivot chord—the last chord which has a diatonic function in both keys. Identification of a pivot chord, therefore, may be a retroactive procedure. Find the triad which is unmistakably in the new key: the pivot chord will be the one directly preceding.

I. Improvising modulations.

The most usual common chords between near-related keys are illustrated in the diagrams below. These are abstract illustrations, drawn to be applicable to any diatonic key relationship. You can make them more specific by substituting a "home" key and listing its near-related keys in the left column. For instance, if you begin in F major, the supertonic key would be G minor. Reading across, the potential common chords would be:

$\frac{\text{ii}}{\text{i}}$ (a g-minor triad), $\frac{\text{IV}}{\text{III}}$ (a B♭-major triad), and $\frac{\text{V}}{\text{IV}}$ (a C-major triad).

These diagrams are somewhat selective, in that not all possible common chord relationships are shown. Included are seventeen modulatory pivots from major keys and fifteen from minor. It will be instructive for you to create your own modulations, experimenting with the alternative common chord possibilities.

From major keys

Related Keys	*Triads*						
	I	ii	iii	IV	V	vi	vii°
Supertonic key		i		III	IV		
Mediant key	VI		i			iv	
Subdominant key		vi		I		iii	
Dominant key	IV		vi		I	ii	
Submediant key		iv		VI		i	ii°

84

From minor keys

Related Keys	Triads							
	i	ii°	III	iv	(IV)	V	VI	vii°
Mediant key	vi	vii°	I	ii			IV	
Subdominant key				i			III	
Dominant key	iv		VI					
Submediant key	iii			vi			I	
Subtonic key	ii		IV		V			

It is possible to expedite the spontaneous improvising of modulations by limiting the common chord vocabulary even further. You will note that the tonic chord appears more frequently as a pivot than any other triad. A simple formula can be suggested which will result in functional, if not always subtle, modulations.

First key: I V I x x
Second key: x I ii⁶ V I

This progression minimally fulfills requirements one and three stated in Project 16—to establish the original and new key centers. There will also be a common chord (requirement 2), appearing at different places in the phrase, depending on the relationship between the keys. Here are four sample modulations on this formula.

Modulations from G major.

Modulations from E minor.

Playing modulations in this way provides an excellent opportunity to concentrate on the aural effect. Retain and compare the two key centers as before. It is also valuable to preconstruct an aural image of the modulation before you play. Play the original tonic, then sing through the chord roots, or the planned melody, before playing the phrase.

II. The modulating phrases which follow are somewhat more elaborate and illustrate additional common chord resources. The signatures may be for either the original or the new key. Play and listen carefully to each phrase; sing the chord roots; identify and analyze the pivot chord.

A. Diatonic modulations from major keys.

B. Diatonic modulations from minor keys.

III. The following melodies illustrate various modulations from major and minor keys. The harmonizations may be worked out in several steps.

1. Sing or play the melody.

2. Study the cadence to determine possible concluding keys.

3. Study the phrase beginnings to determine possible opening keys.

4. Select an appropriate pivot chord.

5. Select remaining harmonies—play soprano and bass.

6. Play the phrase in four-part texture, listening carefully to the modulatory effect.

Some of these melodies may be harmonized in more than one way, i.e., with different modulations, but the keys involved should always be near-related. The signatures may refer to either the original or the new key.

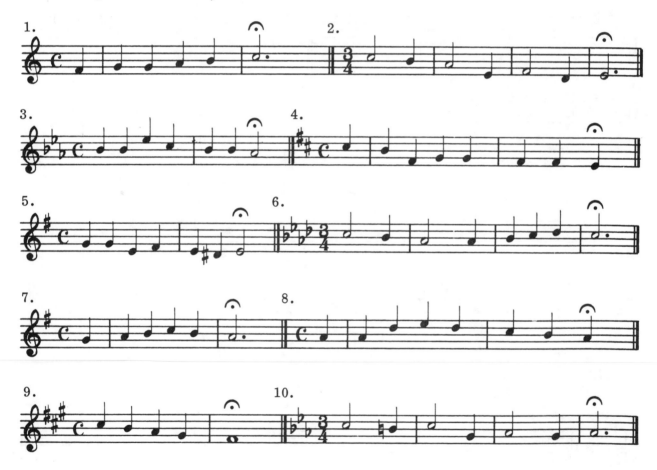

Nonharmonic Tones—Passing and Neighboring Tones

Nonharmonic tones are those which are not members of the prevailing harmony. If a triad consists of the intervals 1-3-5-8 above the bass, the intervening intervals 2-4-6-7-9 will be nonharmonic. Nonharmonic tones are a very common occurrence in all types of music. You have already performed many of these in harmonizing the familiar tunes in previous projects.

I. Identifying nonharmonic tones.

Play these phrases and identify the nonharmonic tones as they appear in either treble or bass parts.

Ex. 18.1. Bach, Four Keyboard works.

1. Menuet

Roots

2. Courante

Roots

3. Menuet

Roots

4. Prelude

The identity of nonharmonic tones is dependent upon their relationship to the harmony, so the selection of harmonizing chords will be decisive in determining which of the tones are harmonic (chord tones) and which are not. The first step, then, is to identify the tones that do not conform to the prevailing chord—as we have just done with the familiar excerpts above.

Nonharmonic tones can be more specifically classified according to the three-note melodic configuration that includes the approach, the nonharmonic tone, and its resolution. In the diagrams below, x represents the nonharmonic tone and o represents the surrounding chord tones. An upward-resolving suspension is often called a retardation.

Approached and resolved by step:

  Passing tone: approached and resolved in the same direction.

  Neighboring tone: approached and resolved in opposite directions.

Approached or resolved by repetition:

  Suspension: approached by repetition, resolved by step.

  Anticipation: approached by step, resolved by repetition.

Approached or resolved by leap:

  Appoggiatura: approached by leap, resolved by step.

  Escape tone: approached by step, resolved by leap.

Other nonharmonic tones:

> *Pedal point*: stationary throughout; most often in the bass, and extending over several beats.

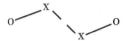

> *Changing tone*: an elaboration of the neighboring tone— a double neighbor.

Refer again to your identification of nonharmonic tones in Exercise I. Compare each melodic situation to the above diagrams and specifically classify each nonharmonic tone.

In chorale style, the presence of nonharmonic material greatly increases the melodic interest of the individual parts and animates the entire texture. Since the hymn melody is a fixed element, the nonharmonic tones are more frequent in alto, tenor, and bass parts.

Passing and neighboring tones most often appear between beats. The passing tone fills in the melodic interval of a third, while the neighboring tone embellishes a repeated note. They may appear in any part, but are especially useful in the bass, enhancing the integrity of this vital outer part. Unaccented nonharmonic tones in the bass usually require no additional figured-bass symbols.

Figured bass numerals for passing and neighboring tones in upper parts indicate the step-wise movement from consonant chord tones above the bass. The distinction between these two non-harmonic tones is made solely on the basis of their resolution; passing tones continue in the same direction, neighboring tones reverse direction.

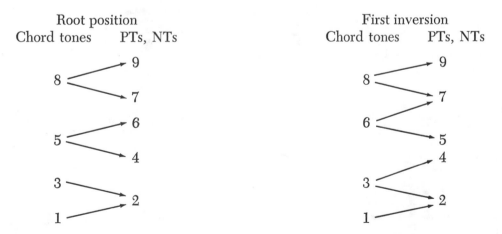

The passing tone is probably the most important of all nonharmonic effects. Of all possibilities, the bass and the 8 − 7 and 6 − 5 passing tones occur most often; the 3 − 2 passing tone is perhaps the least effective. Neighboring tones are somewhat less abundant. Those on *scale degrees* 8 − 7 in any upper part or on 1 − 2 or 5 − 4 in the bass are most useful.

II. Typical settings of passing and neighboring tones.

Nonharmonic tones in the bass are represented by x. As before, the numerals above the line refer to scale degrees in the soprano melody; those below are figured bass symbols measured in intervals above the bass.

Notice the importance of the 6-5, 8-7, and bass passing tones. Neighboring tones conventionally embellish tonic and dominant scale degrees.

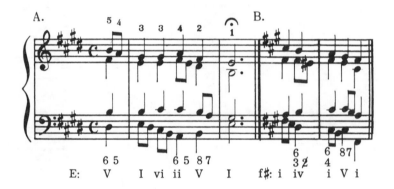

Illustrations:

III. Sequences using passing tones.

Use the natural scale in minor, raising the leading tone only to conclude the phrase.

A. D major

B. E minor

IV. Phrases with figured bass.

Nonharmonic tones should increase, not diminish, the independence of the parts. To this end, the practice of moving from perfect octaves and fifths in contrary or oblique motion should be continued, even when these vertical intervals are created by a nonharmonic tone. The addition of a nonharmonic tone can cause excessive parallelism, but cannot correct an already faulty progression. Situations like the following should be avoided.

Observe the strong downward tendency of 8 − 7 and 6 − 5 figures, and use these as passing, rather than neighboring, tones. The use of nonharmonic tones tends to increase the frequency of alternative doubling and irregular spacing.

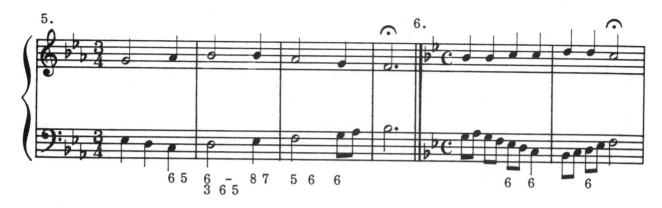

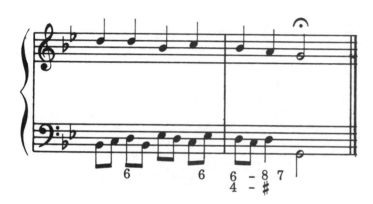

Nonharmonic tones are not the only means for achieving melodic and rhythmic interest. Momentum may also be maintained or generated between beats by changing the doubling, the inversion, or the chord. The latter possibility often creates an ambiguous situation for analysis. Movement between triads with roots a third apart (those having two tones in common) may be variously regarded as either a harmonic change, or simply as the addition of a nonharmonic tone. Most often, the unaccented tones are considered to be nonharmonic, but the final judgment rests in the aural perception of the analyst.

V. Phrases from Bach Chorales.

The chorale harmonizations of J. S. Bach are extremely rich in the imaginative use of nonharmonic material. Play the following phrases, excerpted from the 371 Chorales, and analyze all chords and neighboring and passing tones. Confirm your understanding of these excerpts by transposing each to one or two other keys. Among the devices which appear are double and accented passing tones and accented neighboring tones. The harmonic analysis is given for the effects not yet considered in this text.

3.   No. 135

4.   No. 179

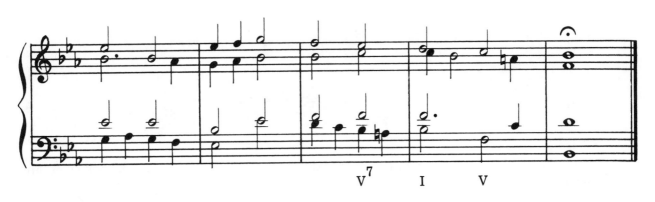

Project 19

Suspension and Anticipation

Suspensions normally occur on the beat, and resolve downward by step. Names for the various suspensions are derived from the intervals formed above the bass: $4-3$, $9-8$, $7-6$, and $2-3$. The $4-3$ and $9-8$ suspensions occur in root position triads, $7-6$ and $2-3$ occur in first inversions, the latter in the bass.

Most frequently it is the leading-tone which is delayed by suspension.

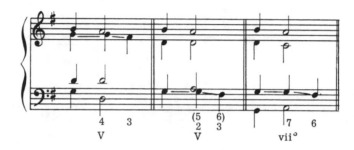

Another common type of suspension affects the tonic scale degree in the tonic triad.

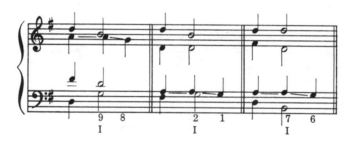

Of the numerous additional possibilities for suspensions on other scale degrees, the following are among the most common.

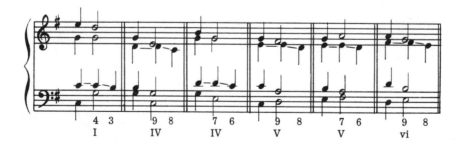

The resolution of a suspension may sometimes be delayed or embellished. Ornamental resolution is particularly idiomatic in the $4-3$ suspension over the dominant. In a $9-8$ suspension, the bass note, or chord, may change simultaneously with the resolution.

The anticipation usually occurs between beats—it moves ahead of the chord change, in contrast to the suspension which lags behind. Typically, the anticipation is used in the soprano part to reinforce a cadence.

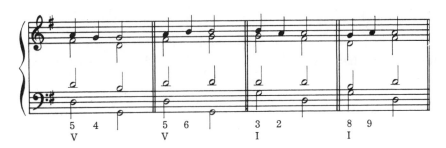

I. Typical settings of suspensions.

Illustrations:

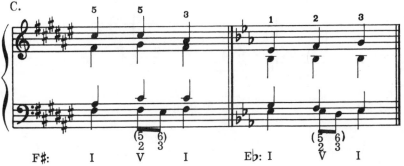

II. Sequence using suspensions.

III. Phrases with figured bass.

Use normal doubling, i.e., the same as if the suspension were not present. Do not double the suspension, but be certain that it is prepared by repetition in the same part. Practice aural discrimination between the various types of suspensions.

IV. Chorale phrases with suspensions.

Play and analyze these excerpts from the Bach Chorales. Transpose each to one or two other keys. Analysis is provided for seventh chords which have not yet been studied.

V. Chorale phrases with appoggiaturas and escape tones.

Appogiaturas and escape tones are used infrequently in chorale texture. The following excerpts illustrate these, as well as passing and neighboring tones, suspensions, and anticipations. Play and analyze.

1. No. 25

2. No. 121   3. No. 149

4. No. 156

Diatonic Seventh Chords
—The Dominant Seventh

Seventh chords are four-tone sonorities consisting of the intervals of third, fifth, and seventh above the root. The usual figured-bass designations are: root position, ^{7}; first inversion, $^6_5$; second inversion, $^4_3$; third inversion, $^4_2$. Two factors determine the classification of seventh-chord types: the type of triad which forms the basis of the chord, and the interval measured from root to seventh. There are five common types:

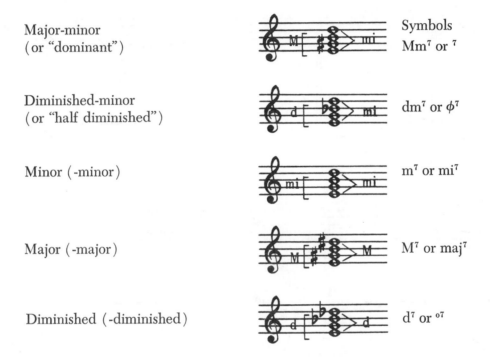

		Symbols
Major-minor (or "dominant")		Mm^7 or ^{7}
Diminished-minor (or "half diminished")		dm^7 or ϕ^7
Minor (-minor)		m^7 or mi^7
Major (-major)		M^7 or maj^7
Diminished (-diminished)		d^7 or $°^7$

I. Diatonic seventh chords.

Play the following seventh chords and analyze the function of each in the indicated key. There should be four different tones in each chord, i.e., no tones doubled. Practice aural discrimination between types of seventh chords. Identify the root and sing each chord ($1 - 3 - 5 - 7 - 5 - 3 - 1$) after playing.

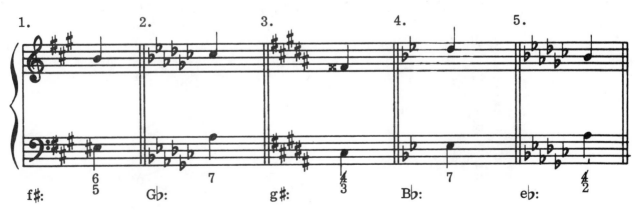

Control of the chord seventh is comparable to certain nonharmonic tone figures, with the added limitation that the seventh virtually always resolves *downward* by step. The four possible preparation figures are:

1. By repetition, as suspension

2. By step, as passing tone

3. By step, as neighboring tone

4. By leap, as appoggiatura

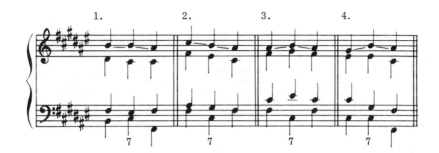

In general, the suspension preparation is the strongest and is appropriate to any seventh chord; the appoggiatura figure has limited application. Nonharmonic tones often create a sonority identical to that of a seventh chord. Analysis is usually determined by rhythmic placement. If the combination of tones occurs on the beat and is heard as an essential harmonic change, it is regarded as a seventh chord.

The Dominant Seventh

Of all seventh chords, that on the dominant is the most common and versatile. It occurs in all inversions and, in various situations, may use any preparation figure. Its harmonic function is equivalent to the dominant triad.

The two famous themes quoted below include melodic outlines of the dominant seventh chord.

Ex. 20.1. Mozart, Eine Kleine Nachtmusik

Ex. 20.2. Haydn, Symphony No. 94, "The Surprise"

II. Typical settings.

In root position, the V^7 may have the root doubled and the fifth omitted. This is illustrated in letter A below. Letter D illustrates the only common situation in which a chord seventh ascends.

A. $\dfrac{3 \quad 4 \quad 4 \quad 3}{\text{I} \quad \text{IV} \quad \text{V}^7 \quad \text{I}}$

B. $\dfrac{3 \quad 2 \quad 1}{\text{I} \quad \text{V}^7 \quad \text{I}}$

C. $\dfrac{3 \quad 4 \quad 3}{\text{I} \quad \text{V}^6_5 \quad \text{I}}$

D. $\dfrac{3 \quad 4 \quad 5 \quad 4 \quad 3}{\text{I} \quad \text{V}^4_3 \quad \text{I}^6 \quad \text{V}^4_3 \quad \text{I}}$

E. $\dfrac{3 \quad 4 \quad 2 \quad 5}{\text{I} \quad \text{IV} \quad \text{V}^4_2 \quad \text{I}^6}$

Illustrations:

III. Phrases with figured bass.

Sing the dominant seventh chords as they appear, and observe the preparation of the chord seventh.

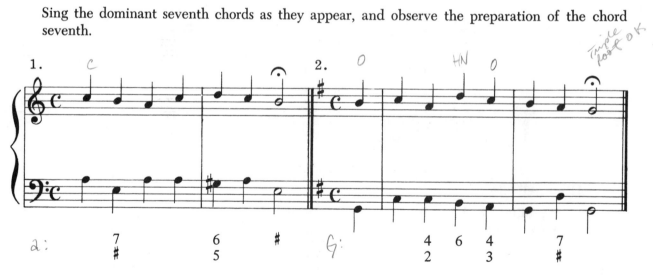

IV. Melody harmonization.

The dominant seventh chord may be used as an alternative to V or vii°, i.e., to harmonize scale degrees 5, 7, 2, or 4. Use all materials previously studied including non-harmonic tones and, in nos. 5 and 6, modulation.

The Supertonic Seventh

The supertonic seventh chord normally progresses to V or V^7; the dominant may be preceded by I_4^6, in which case the seventh of ii^7 is momentarily retained before resolving. Suspension preparation is usually employed.

This chord is most often found in first inversion; rarely in second inversion. In minor keys, root position seldom occurs due to the diminished ii^o present in the chord. In root position (major keys) an incomplete ii^7 may have two thirds and no fifth.

The following examples are from two famous works for piano that begin with a supertonic seventh.

Ex. 21.1. Chopin, Nocturne in B Major, Op. 62.

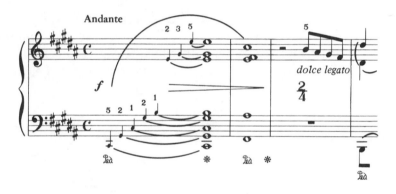

Ex. 21.2. Beethoven, Piano Sonata, Op. 31, No. 3

I. Typical settings.

    Do letter A in major keys only.

    A. $\dfrac{8}{I}\ \dfrac{8}{ii^7}\ \dfrac{7}{V}\ \dfrac{8}{I}$ $\dfrac{3}{I}\ \dfrac{4}{ii^7}\ \dfrac{2}{V}\ \dfrac{3}{I}$

    B. $\dfrac{8}{I}\ \dfrac{8}{ii_5^6}\ \dfrac{7}{V}\ \dfrac{8}{I}$ $\dfrac{3}{I}\ \dfrac{2}{ii_5^6}\ \dfrac{2}{V}\ \dfrac{1}{I}$

    C. $\dfrac{5}{I}\ \dfrac{4}{ii_2^4}\ \dfrac{4}{V_5^6}\ \dfrac{3}{I}$

Illustrations:

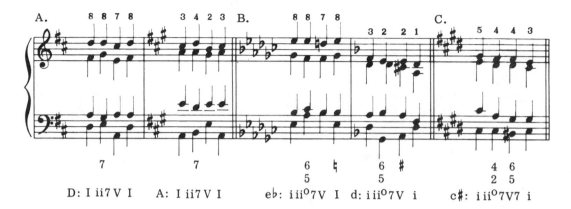

D: I ii7 V I   A: I ii7 V I   e♭: iii°7 V I   d: iii°7 V i   c♯: i ii°7 V7 i

II. The minor seventh and diminished-minor seventh chords.

The minor seventh chord is the least dissonant of all the sevenths, being characterized by its inclusion of two perfect fifths and its lack of a tritone.

The diminished-minor seventh is notably more dissonant and less stable. Its tritone appears in a critical position, above the root, so the identity of the root is obscured. This sonority contains the same intervals as the major-minor seventh, with which it is sometimes confused. A curiosity of the tonal system is that these two seventh chords are mirror images of each other.

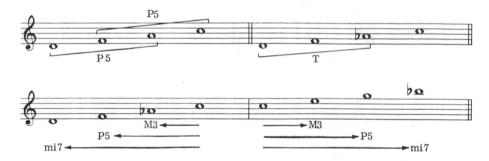

Sing minor and diminished-minor seventh chords, beginning on the root, third, fifth, or seventh.

Intervals, melodic patterns, and chords can often be aurally identified by associating them with music with which you are familiar. Below are some famous musical themes which make vivid use of major-minor, minor, and diminished-minor seventh chords. Search your own musical experience for other examples.

Ex. 21.3. Wagner, *Lohengrin*

Ex. 21.4. Debussy, *La fille aux cheveux de lin*

Copyright 1910 Durand et Cie. Used by permission of the publisher Theodore Presser Company, Sole Representative U.S.A.

Ex. 21.5. Rachmaninoff, Second Piano Concerto

Copyright by Edition Russe de Musique. Copyright assigned to Boosey & Hawkes, Ltd. Reprinted by permission of Boosey & Hawkes, Inc.

III.   Phrases with figured bass.

Sing the supertonic seventh chords.

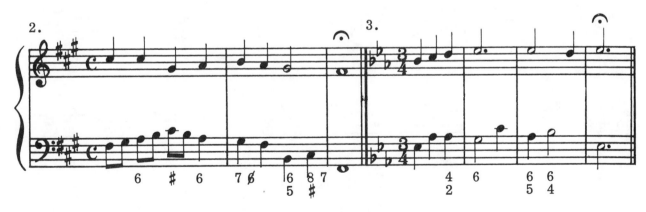

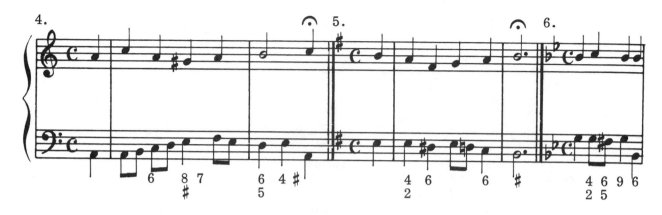

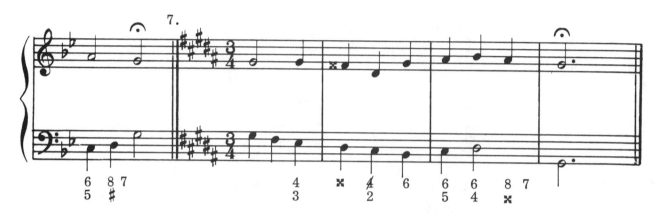

IV. Melody harmonization.

Continue to use nonharmonic tones and chord changes between beats to add rhythmic interest. The progression $ii_5^6 - V$ is especially useful at cadences. Prepare the seventh of ii^7 as a suspension.

The Leading-Tone Seventh

Like the leading-tone triad, this seventh chord is most often preceded by I, ii, or IV, and normally resolves to I.

It is much more common in minor keys than in major. In minor, the leading-tone seventh appears in all inversions and may use any type of preparation for the seventh. This chord consists entirely of active scale degrees. Consequently, all chord members normally resolve by step: 6 to 5, 4 to 3, 2 to 1 or 3, and 7 to 8.

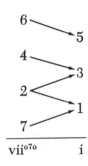

I. Typical settings.

Play these in minor keys only. Observe the stepwise resolution of vii°⁷° in all parts.

A. $\dfrac{3 \quad 4 \quad 3}{\text{i} \quad \text{vii}^{\circ 7 \circ} \quad \text{i}}$ $\dfrac{1 \quad 2 \quad 1}{\text{i} \quad \text{vii}^{\circ 7 \circ} \quad \text{i}}$

C. $\dfrac{8 \quad 7 \quad 8}{\text{i} \quad \text{vii}^{\circ 5} \quad \text{i}^6}$ $\dfrac{3 \quad 4 \quad 3}{\text{i} \quad \text{vii}^{\circ 5} \quad \text{i}^6}$

B. $\dfrac{3 \quad 4 \quad 4 \quad 3}{\text{i} \quad \text{iv} \quad \text{vii}^{\circ 7 \circ} \quad \text{i}}$ $\dfrac{1 \quad 1 \quad 2 \quad 1}{\text{i} \quad \text{iv} \quad \text{vii}^{\circ 7 \circ} \quad \text{i}}$

D. $\dfrac{8 \quad 8 \quad 7 \quad 8}{\text{i} \quad \text{iv} \quad \text{vii}^{\circ 3} \quad \text{i}^6}$ $\dfrac{3 \quad 4 \quad 2 \quad 3}{\text{i} \quad \text{iv} \quad \text{vii}^{\circ 3} \quad \text{i}^6}$

Illustrations:

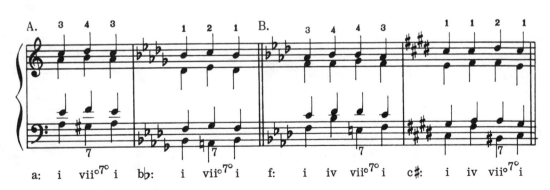

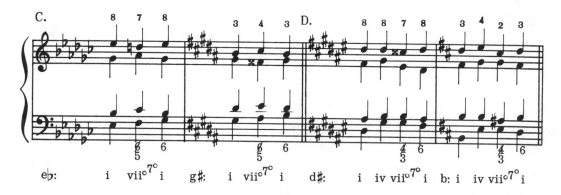

II. The diminished seventh chord.

This chord consists entirely of superimposed minor thirds and is the third sonority we have encountered which divides an octave into equal segments. The tritone, augmented triad, and diminished seventh chord divide the twelve-semitone octave into two, three, and four equal parts.[1]

The diminished seventh chord contains only minor thirds and tritones. Since there are no perfect fifths, the root is indeterminate, and can be positively identified only by the resolution of the chord. Moreover, the sonority often has a transient quality since it is easily transformed into a major-minor or diminished-minor seventh. Lowering any tone of the diminished seventh chord by a half step will create a major-minor seventh; similarly raising any chord tone will create a diminished-minor seventh.

A valuable aural exercise is to play these chromatic changes at the keyboard and to sing the resulting seventh chords. Successively lower and raise each chord member, identify the new root, and sing the chord. One such series is illustrated below; begin also with other diminished seventh chords.

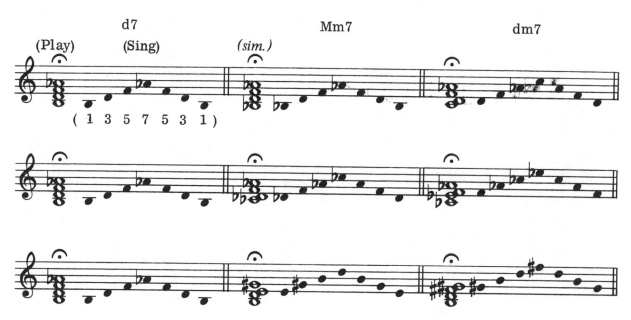

[1]Refer to Appendix 1 for illustrations of these octave divisions.

The sound of the diminished seventh chord is frequently heard in music of the nineteenth century. Because of its versatility it is characteristic of modulating passages, such as transitions and development sections. In a thematic context the sonority may add a special poignancy or drama. The diminished seventh plays an important role in the introduction to Brahms' First Symphony and Dvorak's "New World" Symphony. The diminished-minor seventh is prominent in the Tchaikovsky theme, as well as the diminished seventh. Observe also the use of nonharmonic tones in this excerpt.

Ex. 22.1.   Brahms, Symphony No. 1, Op. 68

Ex. 22.2.   Dvorak, Symphony No. 5, Op. 95

Ex. 22.3.   Tchaikovsky, Sixth Symphony

III. Phrases with figured bass.

Learn to recognize the distinctive dissonance of the diminished seventh chord.

IV. Melody harmonization.

The leading-tone seventh chord most frequently harmonizes scale degrees 2, 4, or 7.

Project 23

The Subdominant Seventh

The theme quoted below opens with the progression iv⁷ − V, in the key of B-flat minor. This movement has also been scored for string orchestra and is well known under the title "Adagio for Strings".

Ex. 23.1. Samuel Barber, String Quartet, Op. 11

"String Quartet, Op. 11" Copyright © 1943 by G. Schirmer, Inc. Used by permission.

The IV⁷ is a major seventh chord in major keys and may be a minor or major-minor seventh chord in minor keys—using either the natural or the raised sixth scale degree. It normally progresses to a dominant triad, but may move to I$_4^6$ or be interposed between I$_4^6$ and V. Suspension preparation is usual for the chord seventh.

In root position the major seventh and minor seventh chords contain two perfect fifths. The progression IV⁷ − V requires that one of these be left in similar motion, with the leap of a fifth occurring in one of the inner parts. The chord fifth of V is most often doubled, and this situation creates an opportunity for melodic embellishment of the dominant harmony. The subdominant seventh seldom progresses directly to V⁷ since in this case the seventh of V⁷ is prepared by leap from above.

I. Typical settings.

Play in all major and minor keys.

A.
$$\frac{3 \quad 3 \quad 2 \quad 1}{\text{I} \quad \text{IV}^7 \quad \text{V} \quad \text{I}}$$

B.
$$\frac{5 \quad 4 \quad 4 \quad 3}{\text{I} \quad \text{IV}^6_5 \quad \text{V}^6_5 \quad \text{I}}$$

Illustrations: The first setting (letter A) is shown in several keys to demonstrate various embellishments of the dominant triad.

II. The major seventh chord.

The unique feature of this sonority is the presence of the interval of the major seventh or its inversion, the minor second. This dissonance appears in no other conventional triad or seventh chord. The two perfect fifths in this chord lend a degree of similarity to the minor seventh chord.

1. Sing major and minor seventh *intervals* (1-7) above a given root.

2. Sing major and minor seventh *chords* in the order 1-5-3-7, emphasizing the two perfect fifths.

3. Sing major seventh chords beginning with the root, third, fifth, or seventh.

The sound of the major seventh chord is frequently heard in jazz and popular music. Two popular songs which begin with a major seventh chord are "Dancing in the Dark" and "Talk of the Town". The major seventh may also be an "added note", included to enrich or color the chord.

The tonic triad, with added major seventh is a common cadential effect. In these examples the dominant seventh chord is shown with some typical chromatic alterations.

III.   Phrases with figured bass.

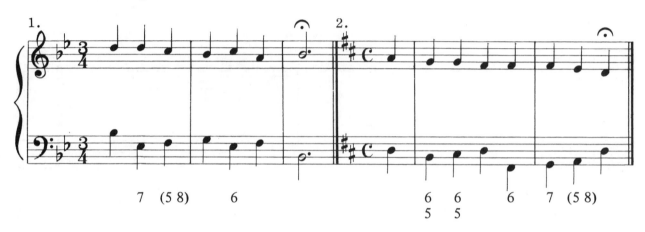

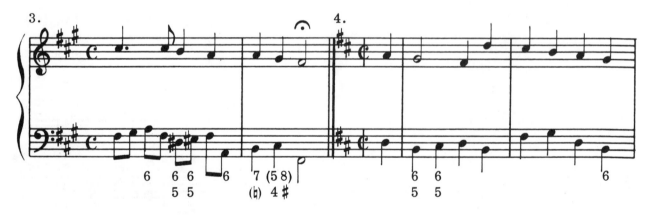

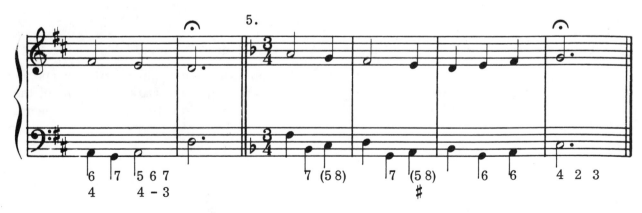

IV. Melody harmonization.

Use IV⁷ in root position to harmonize the third scale degree and in first inversion to harmonize the fourth scale degree. Prepare the chord seventh as a suspension.

Project 24

The Submediant, Tonic, and Mediant Sevenths

The seventh chord on the submediant is a minor seventh in major keys and most frequently occurs as a diminished-minor seventh (with the raised sixth degree) in minor. It is commonly preceded by I or iii, and progresses to ii or ii⁷, or V⁶₅. The tonic seventh chord may be used as an alternative to iii in harmonizing the descending leading-tone: I (or I⁶) — I⁷ — IV — I. The mediant seventh is generally limited to major keys and normally progresses to vi or vi⁷. To establish suspension preparation for the chord seventh, it may be preceded by ii⁶.

I. Typical settings.

Do letters A and D in major keys only. Resolve all chord sevenths downward by step. In a series of seventh chords this is accomplished by varying the doubling. Alternate seventh chords are incomplete, having either the chord root or third doubled.

$$\text{A.} \quad \frac{5 \quad 5 \quad 4 \quad 4 \quad 3}{\text{I} \quad \text{vi}^7 \quad \text{ii}^7 \quad \text{V}^7 \quad \text{I}}$$

$$\text{B.} \quad \frac{5 \quad 5 \quad 4 \quad 3}{\text{I} \quad \text{vi}^7 \quad \text{V}^6_{|5} \quad \text{I}}$$

$$\text{C.} \quad \frac{8 \quad 7 \quad 6 \quad 5}{\text{I} \quad \text{I}^7 \quad \text{IV} \quad \text{I}}$$

$$\text{D.} \quad \frac{3 \quad 4 \quad 5 \quad 5 \quad 4 \quad 4 \quad 3}{\text{I} \quad \text{ii}^6 \quad \text{iii}^7 \quad \text{vi}^7 \quad \text{ii}^7 \quad \text{V}^7 \quad \text{I}}$$

Illustrations:

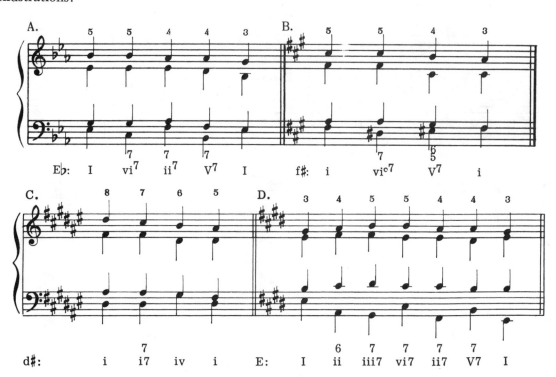

II. Sequences.

We have seen that tonality is most emphatically expressed through harmonic progressions in descending fifths. Diatonic seventh chords may be used effectively in such sequences, in addition to the typical settings already considered.

Every diatonic scale contains at least one "imperfect" fifth (diminished fifth or augmented fourth) and one diminished triad. A complete cycle of fifth-related triads then would include a diminished triad in root position and possibly one or more augmented leaps—conditions usually avoided, but partially mitigated by the compelling momentum of the sequence. The subtonic triad appears in minor keys.

The two conventional systems of chord designation are included with these illustrations. One is a functional system in which numerals indicate the relation of a chord to the key center. The "lead sheet" method, commonly found in popular music, indicates chord roots by capital letters. Both systems also designate chord types—the first by upper- and lowercase Roman numerals and the superscript symbols ° and ⁺, the second by adding qualifying letters and/or symbols. Refer back to Project 20 for the equivalent seventh-chord designations in the two systems.

Neither of these methods is perfect in its discrimination of chord types, and the more complex the harmony, the more cumbersome is the symbolic designation. Also, neither method is fully standardized. Many small variances in symbols and nomenclature may be encountered.

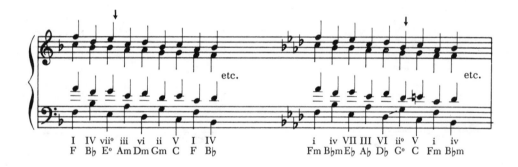

The addition of passing tones creates seventh-chord sonorities between beats. The doubling is adjusted (alternate triads incomplete) to accommodate the resolutions of the passing tones.

In a series of diatonic seventh chords each chord seventh is prepared by repetition. Alternate chords appear with the third doubled.

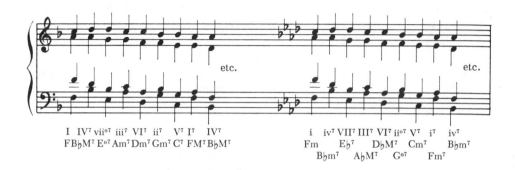

By using inversions, these series may be achieved with step-wise motion in all parts. The sequence may, of course, be altered or interrupted at any point; or, by adding simple chromatic alterations, a modulation may be accomplished. Chord designations remain the same regardless of inversions.

III. Phrases with figured bass.

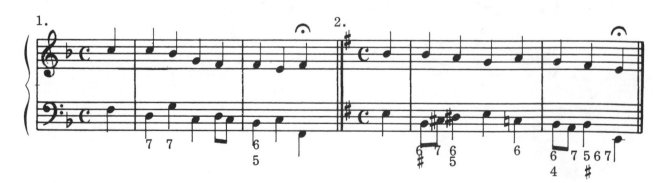

IV. Melody harmonization.

Use vi⁷ or iii⁷ to harmonize the fifth scale degree and I⁷ to harmonize the descending leading-tone.

Project 25

Review: Melody Harmonization
with Diatonic Seventh Chords

The principles of root relationship summarized in Project 15 apply to seventh chords as well as triads. Progressions by descending fifths are even more strongly indicated when one or more seventh chords are used. A complete series of fifth-related diatonic seventh chords is illustrated below.

I^7	IV^7	vii^{o7}	iii^7	vi^7	ii^7	V^7	I

Seventh chords on the tonic, subdominant, and leading-tone more often occur in alternate positions in the series. Arrows indicate the most common progressions—usually by root movement in descending fifths.

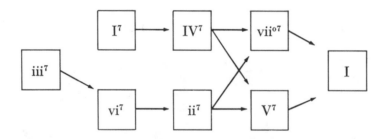

With the addition of modulation, nonharmonic tones, and seventh chords to the vocabulary, melody harmonization becomes increasingly sophisticated. The process may still be accomplished in four general steps, but with more options available in each.

1. *Determine the key.* Several additional cadence formulas are available: V^7 and vii^{o7o} may be used in authentic cadences, ii^7 and IV^7 may precede V at half cadences. The progression $ii_5^6 - V (-I)$ is particularly appropriate at cadence points. The cadence chord is usually a triad in root position (I, V, or vi) but may be embellished with a suspension or anticipation. Modulation should be employed frequently to keep the chorale melody in the lower tetrachord of the prevailing scale.

2. *Select appropriate triads—or seventh chords.* Generally, a seventh chord may substitute at any point for its functionally equivalent triad. In chorale harmonizations, seventh chords more often appear singly than in consecutive sequence. Of all diatonic sevenths, those on the dominant and supertonic and the leading-tone in minor are most common and useful.

3. *Refine the bass line.* Use inversions and passing tones to impart melodic interest to the bass. The V^7 and vii^{o7o} (in minor) may be used in any inversion; ii^7 and IV^7 seldom appear in second inversion; the remaining seventh chords are generally restricted to root position—and major keys.

4. *Add inner parts.* The skillful and imaginative use of nonharmonic tones (especially suspensions) in the alto and tenor parts contributes immeasurably to the overall artistic effect. Vitalize the harmonic rhythm also by changing the doubling, the inversion, or the chord between beats. Prepare and resolve all chord sevenths. Suspension preparation is the strongest and is appropriate to all seventh chords. Passing-tone preparation may be used in any instances of chord repetition. Other preparation figures are generally applicable only to V^7 and $vii^{o7°}$.

Analytical Considerations

It has been observed that identical vertical sonorities may be created by using either nonharmonic tones or seventh chords. For purposes of analysis, the distinction may be made on the basis of the rhythmic situation, with the nonharmonic tone occupying the weaker position.

Incomplete seventh chords may be momentarily identical to triads with suspensions. Analysis is based primarily on the manner of resolution.

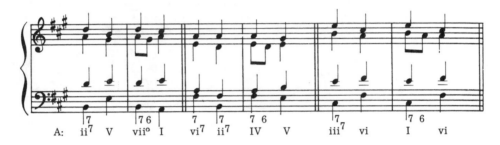

Each of the seven diatonic tones of a major or minor scale can serve as the root, third, fifth, or seventh of a seventh chord. With seven tones fulfilling as many as twenty-eight harmonic roles, it is obvious that there is considerable overlapping of notes between consecutive seventh chords. The examples in Project 24 illustrated that fifth-related seventh chords have two tones in common. Seventh chords with roots a third apart have three common tones. Moving only one tone in such progressions creates little feeling of advancing the tonal movement toward the tonic.

I. Chorales with unfigured bass.

   The following are taken from the collection of 371 Chorale Harmonizations by J. S. Bach. Play the bass and soprano lines separately, singing the other part as you play. These two most prominent parts form quite a complete and satisfactory duet in themselves, even without the inner voices. It is very instructive to study this two-voice framework in terms of contrapuntal motion (contrary, oblique, similar, parallel), the vertical intervals, and their harmonic implications. The first three steps in harmonization have largely been accomplished; only step four, the addition of alto and tenor parts, remains. Play these chorales, adding the missing voices and including suspensions and passing tones as appropriate.

1. No. 110, phrases 1, 2, 5 & 6.

2. No. 157

3. No. 192

4. No. 95

II. Chorale melodies.

Harmonize in four parts including modulation, nonharmonic tones and diatonic seventh chords. Keep in mind the four general steps suggested for melody harmonization. It is sometimes advantageous to determine harmonizations for the cadences first.

1. No. 151.

The four cadences in this chorale could be harmonized in several near-related keys as follows:

Measures	Keys	Scale degrees
2	G	4 - 3
"	C	8 - 7
4-5	G	2 - 1
"	e	4 - 3
7	G	8 - 7
"	D	4 - 3
"	e	3 - 2
9	G	2 - 1

2. No. 12

3. No. 22, phrases 1, 2, 5, & 6

Unit III
Chromatic Harmony

Introduction to Secondary Dominants

Traditional harmonic materials may be classified in two broad categories, diatonic and chromatic. Diatonic chords—using only the tones available in the major scale, or any of the three forms of minor—have been the subject of the preceding studies. Chromaticism results from the alteration of one or more tones of a diatonic scale or chord. The resources of chromatic harmony are virtually equal in extent and variety to those of the diatonic materials; thus, the addition of chromatically altered chords expands the harmonic vocabulary almost two-fold.

Play this famous theme, and observe which of the chords do not conform to the D-flat major scale.

Ex. 26.1. Tchaikovsky, Piano Concerto in B-flat Minor

By far the largest family of altered chords come under a general classification as secondary dominants.[1] In this context the term, dominant, is extended to include all triads and seventh chords which normally progress directly to the tonic. Because of their vital role in establishing a key center, these chords may be considered "primary" dominants. (The diminished-minor vii°⁷ occurs relatively infrequently as either a primary or secondary dominant.)

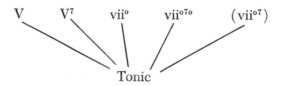

[1]Scholars have advanced various rationales to explain the origin or function of altered chords. Consequently, the student may encounter diverse terms and symbols as his study of harmony proceeds. It is important to understand that such varying concepts are not necessarily contradictory nor mutually exclusive. No single abstract system can serve to perfectly define every musical event; different concepts may be appropriate to different situations, and the mature analyst will learn to build upon several ideas in developing his own insights into musical experience. The terms used in this book have been chosen because they are reasonable and are perhaps the most widely used and understood. The student is encouraged to investigate other options.

Diatonic chords are always defined by their relationship to the tonic center. The designations are customarily abbreviated, but the implied analysis could be stated as V of I, ii of I etc. Any diatonic major or minor triad may momentarily function as a tonic if it is preceded by its own dominant—one of the chord types indicated above: M, Mm⁷, d, d⁷, dm⁷. These temporary dominants are in a secondary position since they are once-removed from the tonal center; their tonal identity is affirmed through their relationship to a diatonic triad. As with diatonic chords, the analysis of secondary dominants is determined by the key in which they occur. In these examples read / as "of," e.g., V *of* V.

G: V   I   C: V   V   I   a: V   i   G: V   ii   V   I   C: V   vi   ii   V   I
              ————   ————   ————   ————
               V/   V/   V/   V/

A complete catalog of all potential secondary dominants could theoretically be developed by relating the five dominant chord types to all diatonic major and minor triads. A systematic study of all fifty possibilities is not to be undertaken here, since many of these potential secondary dominants occur very infrequently. The secondary dominants included in this and subsequent projects are indicated by asterisks in the diagrams below. The Mm⁷ and d⁷ are the most common chord types in this harmonic category. Secondary dominants appear somewhat more frequently in major keys than in minor.

	Major Keys						*Minor Keys*				
	V/	V⁷/	vii°/	vii°⁷/	vii°⁷⁰/		V/	V⁷/	vii°/	vii°⁷/	vii°⁷⁰/
V	✱	✱	✱	✱	✱	v	✱	✱	✱		✱
IV		✱				iv		✱			✱
ii	✱	✱	✱		✱	VI					
vi	✱	✱	✱		✱	III					
iii						VII					

I. Secondary dominants:

Play the following chords and analyze in the designated keys. The analysis of secondary dominants is in two parts: (1) the chord type, represented by one of the five dominant numerals and (2) the diatonic triad to which it is related.

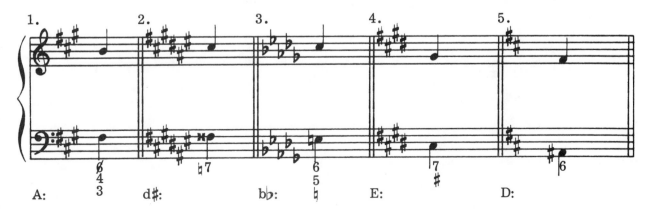

1.   2.   3.   4.   5.

A: d♯:   b♭:   E: D:
      6   6   7   6
      4   ♮7   5
      3   ♮

All altered chords, including secondary dominants, are closely related to their diatonic counterparts. Each may be derived by the chromatic alteration of one or more tones of a diatonic chord.

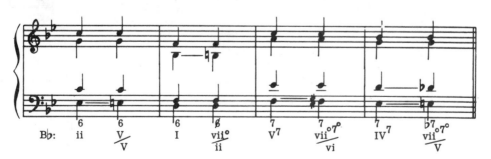

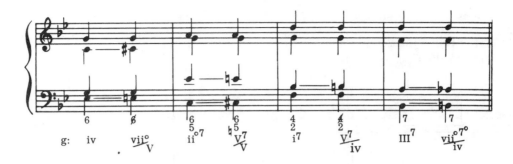

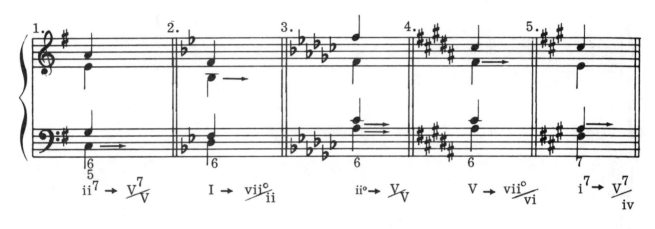

II. Chromatic alterations of diatonic chords.

Play each diatonic chord and then change it to a secondary dominant by chromatically altering one or two tones. The two chords in such diatonic-chromatic pairs may be used interchangeably in harmonization; observe carefully the variance in the aural effect and learn to recognize secondary dominant sonorities.

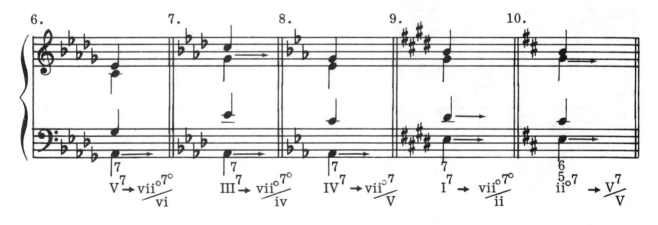

III.   Progressions with figured bass.

Each of the following progressions begins with a secondary dominant. Play and analyze; sing the chord roots or the bass tones as you play.

Secondary Dominants of the Dominant

These secondary dominants are derived through the chromatic alteration of the chords that normally progress directly to the dominant triad—ii, ii⁷, IV, IV⁷. They are characterized by the presence of the raised fourth scale degree; in minor keys the raised sixth degree accompanies the raised fourth, and the lowered third degree is sometimes used in major. This group of chromatic chords relate to their diatonic counterparts as follows:

	Major Keys	*Minor Keys*
V of V	ii (♯4)	ii° (♯4, ♯6)
V⁷ of V	ii⁷ (♯4)	ii°⁷ (♯4, ♯6)
vii° of V	IV (♯4)	iv (♯4, ♯6)
vii°⁷° of V	IV⁷ (♯4, ♭3)	iv⁷ (♯4, ♯6)
vii°⁷ of V	IV⁷ (♯4)	- - - - - - - - -

These chords usually resolve to V; I⁶₄ may be interposed before this resolution. They are commonly preceded by the tonic triad; also by vi, ii or IV. The raised fourth (a temporary leading-tone) most often appears in the bass.

The secondary dominant family presents no chord types that have not been studied before. The five dominant chord types, however, are located in different functional positions within a key. The major-minor seventh and diminished seventh sonorities are probably the most important in this group. Review these chords aurally by singing (1-3-5-7-5-3-1), beginning on the chord root, third, fifth, or seventh.

Major-minor and diminished seventh chords are characterized by the intervals of a tritone and a diminished seventh. To establish these intervals in a tonal position as secondary dominants, sing the following patterns beginning with various pitches as tonic.

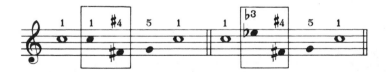

I. Typical settings.

A. $\dfrac{3 \quad 2 \quad 2 \quad 1}{\text{I} \quad \text{V}^6/_\text{v} \quad \text{V} \quad \text{I}}$

B. $\dfrac{8 \quad 8 \quad 7 \quad 8}{\text{I} \quad \underset{6}{\text{V}^5/_\text{v}} \quad \text{V} \quad \text{I}}$ $\qquad$ $\dfrac{3 \quad 2 \quad 2 \quad 1}{\text{I} \quad \underset{6}{\text{V}^5/_\text{v}} \quad \text{V} \quad \text{I}}$

C. $\dfrac{8 \quad 8 \quad 7 \quad 8}{\text{I} \quad \text{vii}^{o6}/_\text{v} \quad \text{V} \quad \text{I}}$ $\qquad$ $\dfrac{5 \quad 6 \quad 7 \quad 8}{\text{I} \quad \text{vii}^{o6}/_\text{v} \quad \text{V} \quad \text{I}}$

D. $\dfrac{8 \quad 8 \quad 7 \quad 8}{\text{I} \quad \text{vii}^{o7o}/_\text{v} \quad \text{V} \quad \text{I}}$ $\qquad$ $\dfrac{3 \quad 3 \quad 2 \quad 1}{\text{I} \quad \text{vii}^{o7o}/_\text{v} \quad \text{V} \quad \text{I}}$

E. $\dfrac{3 \quad 3 \quad 2 \quad 1}{\text{I} \quad \text{vii}^{o7}/_\text{v} \quad \text{V} \quad \text{I}}$ $\quad$ (major keys only)

Illustrations:

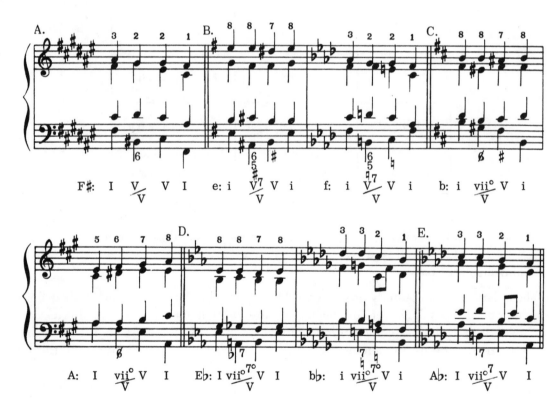

Here are two examples of secondary dominants of V from music literature. The Mozart excerpt illustrates the normal resolution through I$^6_4$ to V. The passage from "Death and Transfiguration" is a particularly memorable application of V^7/v, but without resolution to the dominant. Two other altered chords also appear in this passage.

Ex. 27.1. Mozart, Piano Sonata, K. 311

Ex. 27.2. Richard Strauss, Death and Transfiguration

Copyright 1904 by C. F. Peters, in all Berne Convention countries.

II. Phrases with figured bass.

The altered tones should not be doubled; also avoid leaps of an augmented 4th or 2nd, especially in the bass. The progression vii°^{7}/v — V is scored as the diatonic version IV^7 — V, i.e., with a leap in one of the inner parts to avoid parallelism. These secondary dominants generally occur as alternatives to their diatonic counterparts, but also have a unique function in harmonizing altered tones in the melodic line, as in nos. 7, 8, and 9 below. The raised fourth degree occasionally resolves chromatically downward to the chord seventh of V^7.

III. Melody harmonization.

Secondary dominants of V are most often used to harmonize scale degrees 1, 2, or 3. Thus, they may substitute for ii, ii⁷, IV, or IV⁷ except when the diatonic fourth scale degree appears in the soprano. The raised fourth degree, or the lowered third in major, requires the use of the secondary dominant. Employ at least one secondary dominant of the dominant in each of these melodies.

Project 28

Secondary Dominants of the Subdominant

These chords are characterized by their use of the lowered seventh (subtonic) scale degree; in minor keys the raised third degree is also present. Common usage is limited to $V^7/_{IV}$ (Mm^7) and, in minor, $vii^{o7o}/_{iv}$ (d^7). This is the only group of secondary dominants which have wider application than their diatonic relatives, I^7 and III^7. In general they may serve as alternatives to the tonic triad when the progression is to the subdominant.

	Major Keys	*Minor keys*
V^7 of IV	I^7 ($\flat 7$)	i^7 ($\sharp 3$)
vii^{o7o} of iv	– – – –	III^7 ($\sharp 3, \flat 2$)

Sing the following patterns in various keys.

I. Typical settings.

A.
$$\frac{8}{I} \quad \frac{8}{V^4_2/_{IV}} \quad \frac{8}{IV^6} \quad \frac{7}{V} \quad \frac{8}{I} \qquad \frac{5}{I} \quad \frac{5}{V^4_2/_{IV}} \quad \frac{4}{IV^6} \quad \frac{2}{V} \quad \frac{3}{I}$$

B.
$$\frac{8}{I} \quad \frac{8}{V^6_5/_{IV}} \quad \frac{8}{IV} \quad \frac{7}{V} \quad \frac{8}{I} \qquad \frac{3}{I} \quad \frac{5}{V^6_5/_{IV}} \quad \frac{4}{IV} \quad \frac{2}{V} \quad \frac{3}{I}$$

C.
$$\frac{5}{i} \quad \frac{5}{vii^{o7o}/_{iv}} \quad \frac{4}{iv} \quad \frac{3}{vii^{o7o}/_{v}} \quad \frac{2}{V} \quad \frac{1}{i} \qquad \text{(minor keys only)}$$

Illustrations:

V^7 of IV appears in the opening themes of two Mozart sonatas.

Ex. 28.1.   Mozart, Piano Sonata, K. 280

Allegro assai

Ex. 28.2.   Mozart, Piano Sonata, K. 332

Allegro

Beethoven's first Symphony actually begins with V⁷/IV—the work is in the key of C major.

Ex. 28.3.   Beethoven, Symphony No. 1, Op. 21

II.   Phrases with figured bass.

Several additional uses for secondary dominants of IV are illustrated in these phrases, including direct chromaticism in the bass and in the soprano, deceptive resolution to ii, and half cadence on IV. Sing the chord roots as you play.

III. Melody harmonization.

Use at least one secondary dominant of IV in each phrase; arrows suggest their placement in the first three. Play each melody slowly before harmonizing and try to mentally project the chord sounds.

Secondary Dominants of the Supertonic

The use of these secondary dominants is generally limited to major keys. The characteristic alteration, raised first scale degree, typically appears in the bass.

Major Keys

V of ii	vi ($\sharp 1$)
V^7 of ii	vi^7 ($\sharp 1$)
$vii°$ of ii	I ($\sharp 1$)
$vii°^{7°}$ of ii	I^7 ($\sharp 1, \flat 7$)

Sing these patterns in various keys.

I. Typical settings.

Play these progressions in various major keys, using scale degrees 3 or 5 in the soprano melody with the secondary dominant.

$$
\begin{array}{c}
\quad\;\; (5 \qquad 6) \\
3 \quad\;\; 3 \qquad 4 \quad 2 \quad 3 \\
\hline
\text{A.} \quad \text{I} \quad V^6/_{ii} \quad \text{ii} \quad \text{V} \quad \text{I}
\end{array}
$$

$$
\begin{array}{c}
\qquad\;\; (5) \\
3 \quad\;\; 3 \qquad 4 \quad 2 \quad 3 \\
\hline
\text{B.} \quad \text{I} \quad V^6_5/_{ii} \quad \text{ii} \quad \text{V} \quad \text{I}
\end{array}
$$

$$
\begin{array}{c}
\qquad\;\; (5) \\
3 \quad\;\; 3 \qquad 4 \quad 2 \quad 3 \\
\hline
\text{C.} \quad \text{I} \quad vii°^6/_{ii} \quad \text{ii} \quad \text{V} \quad \text{I}
\end{array}
$$

$$
\begin{array}{c}
\qquad\;\; (5) \\
3 \quad\;\; 3 \qquad 4 \quad 2 \quad 3 \\
\hline
\text{D.} \quad \text{I} \quad vii°^{7°}/_{ii} \quad \text{ii} \quad \text{V} \quad \text{I}
\end{array}
$$

Illustrations:

Here are two famous musical passages that include secondary dominants of ii. The Chopin theme includes a secondary dominant of V (identified by the raised fourth scale degree, a-natural), as well as a secondary dominant of ii (with the raised tonic degree, e-natural). Measures three and four are a transposed re-statement of mm. one and two. The dominant and secondary dominant chords in mm. one and three are characterized by the interval between the lowest and highest parts—an octave plus a sixth or a thirteenth.

Ex. 29.1. Chopin, Ballade, Op. 23

Ex. 29.2. Schubert, "Unfinished" Symphony

II. Phrases with figured bass.

Sing the bass line as you play.

III. Melody harmonization.

Secondary dominants of ii most often harmonize diatonic scale degrees 3 or 5 (occasionally 6) and resolve to ii with the fourth scale degree in the soprano. In a chromatic melody these chords may accommodate the raised first scale degree.

Secondary Dominants of the Submediant

These secondary dominants, like those relating to the supertonic, are also generally limited to major keys.

Major Keys

V of vi	iii ($\sharp$5)
V^7 of vi	iii^7 ($\sharp$5)
vii^{o7o} of vi	V^7 ($\sharp$5)

The characteristic raised fifth scale degree is most often in the bass; approached by leap from above or chromatically from below. In the former situation an accented passing tone figure in the bass is especially appropriate. More frequently than other secondary dominants, V of vi resolves deceptively—to IV or IV^6.

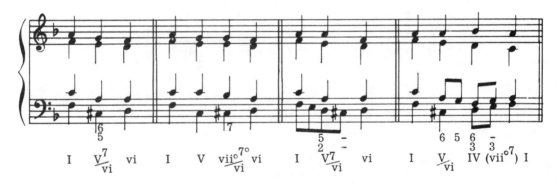

Practice singing these melodic patterns in various major keys.

I. Typical settings.
   Play in various major keys.

A. $\dfrac{3}{I} \quad \dfrac{3}{V^6/_{vi}} \quad \dfrac{1}{vi} \quad \dfrac{2}{ii} \quad \dfrac{7}{V} \quad \dfrac{1}{I}$

B. $\dfrac{3}{1} \quad \dfrac{3}{V^6/_{vi}} \quad \dfrac{4}{IV^6} \quad \dfrac{-}{(vii^{o7})} \quad \dfrac{3}{I}$

C. $\dfrac{3}{I} \quad \dfrac{2}{V^6_5/_{vi}} \quad \dfrac{1}{vi} \quad \dfrac{2}{ii} \quad \dfrac{7}{V} \quad \dfrac{1}{I}$

D. $\dfrac{3}{I} \quad \dfrac{2}{vii^{o7o}/_{vi}} \quad \dfrac{1}{vi} \quad \dfrac{2}{ii} \quad \dfrac{7}{V} \quad \dfrac{1}{I}$

Illustrations:

Several applications of secondary dominants of vi are illustrated in the following famous themes.

Ex. 30.1.   Beethoven, Symphony No. 5, Op. 67

Ex. 30.2.   Beethoven, Piano Sonata, Op. 53

II. Sequences.

Series of fifth-related secondary dominants are quite common in all types of music. Refer again to the Tchaikovsky theme quoted in Project 26; here is an additional example.

Ex. 30.3. Mozart, Piano Sonata, K. 283

The basic series, using only major triads, would appear as follows:

	V	V	V	V	I	IV	V	I
I	/vi	/ii	/V					
F	A	D	G	C	F	B♭	C	F

Secondary dominant sevenths result from the addition of passing tones. The chord, b♭ — d — f — a♭, in this example should be analyzed as a borrowed chord (see Project 31) rather than a secondary dominant.

In the following setting the chord sevenths are approached chromatically. The altered tones progress contrary to their natural tendency.

	V⁷	V⁷	V⁷	V⁷	V⁷	IV⁷	V	I
I	/vi	/ii	/V		/IV			
F	A⁷	D⁷	G⁷	C⁷	F⁷	B♭⁷	C	F

Inversions allow for stepwise motion in all parts.

The preceding progressions illustrate the most common secondary dominants. This vocabulary could be extended in two ways.

A secondary dominant of iii (vii°⁷, with raised second scale degree) might be added to the chain, perhaps by approaching it from vii°⁷ of V.

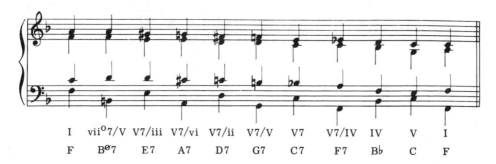

In minor keys the major-minor sevenths, IV⁷ and VII⁷, are diatonic chords. A V⁷ of VI in minor requires the use of the lowered second scale degree—g-flat in the example below. To avoid the tritone root movement between ii° and V, the lower second may be retained in the supertonic, creating a major triad. This special chord is called the Neapolitan triad (abbr. N) and will be considered again in a later project. The tritone root movement now appears between N and V.

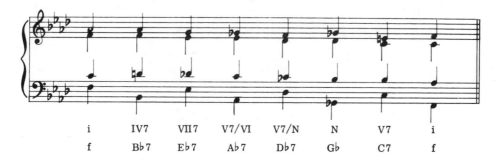

III. Phrases with figured bass.

Secondary dominants of V, IV, and ii are also included. Analyze carefully, designating the specific chord type (vii°⁷° of —, V⁷ of —, etc.) for each secondary dominant. The last two phrases illustrate additional secondary dominants (of iii in major and of VII in minor) which are occasionally encountered.

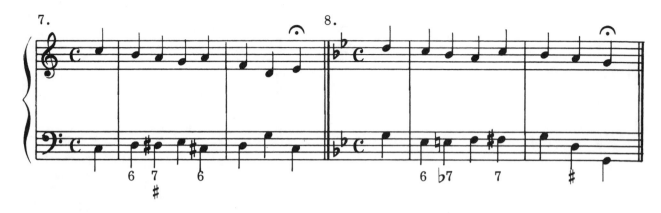

IV. Melody harmonization.

Secondary dominants of vi typically harmonize scale degrees 2 or 3, but may also be used in connection with the chromatically raised fifth degree.

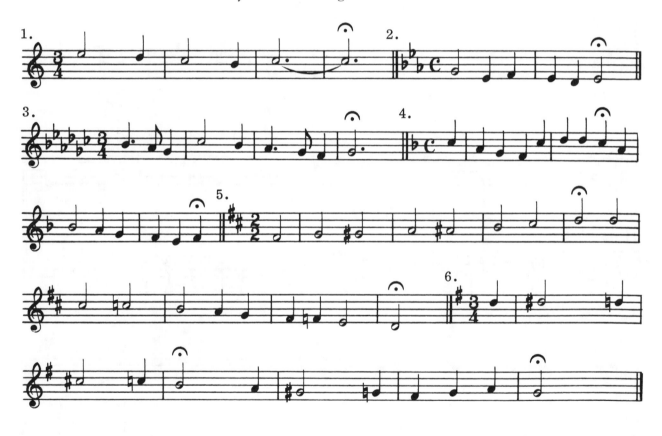

Borrowed Chords

Minor mode, using any of three possible scale forms, is considerably richer than major in *diatonic* chord structures. This imbalance is somewhat offset by the more frequent use of certain *chromatic* materials (e.g. secondary dominants of ii and vi) in major keys. The use of chromatic alteration tends to blur the distinction between parallel major and minor tonalities, since altered chords are often identical in either mode (e.g., secondary dominants of V and IV). An additional step in this mixing of the modes is the use of the lowered sixth or third scale degrees in major. Chords containing these alterations are said to be borrowed—by major, from minor. The possibilities are as follows:

1. Lowered sixth: vii°⁷°, iv, ii°, ii°⁷.
2. Lowered third: IV⁷.
3. Lowered sixth and third: VI.

Probably the most important of these are the vii°⁷° (diminished seventh) and iv (minor). The lowered sixth scale degree most strongly characterizes borrowed chords; it requires a descending resolution, and is most often approached by half step from above or below.

The following is a vivid example of the use of the lowered sixth in a major key.

Ex. 31.1. Schumann, *Ich grolle nicht* from Dichterliebe, Op. 28.

I. Typical settings.

These are similar to the settings of vii°⁷° in Project 22, except for the change of mode. The first three settings may be played with or without the subdominant triad. Play in major keys.

A.	3	(4)	4	3	1	(1)	2	1
	I	(IV)	vii°⁷°	I	I	(IV)	vii°⁷°	I
B.	8	(8)	7	8	3	(4)	4	3
	I	(IV)	vii°⁰⁶₅	I⁶	I	(IV)	vii°⁰⁶₅	I⁶

C.

$$\frac{8}{I} \quad \frac{(8)}{(IV)} \quad \frac{7}{vii^{o4}_{3}} \quad \frac{8}{I^{6}} \qquad \frac{3}{I} \quad \frac{(4)}{(IV)} \quad \frac{2}{vii^{o4}_{3}} \quad \frac{3}{I^{6}}$$

D.

$$\frac{3}{I} \quad \frac{4}{V^{4}_{2}/iv} \quad \frac{3}{IV^{6}_{iv6}} \quad \frac{2}{I^{6}_{4}} \quad \frac{1}{V} \qquad \frac{}{I}$$

Illustrations:

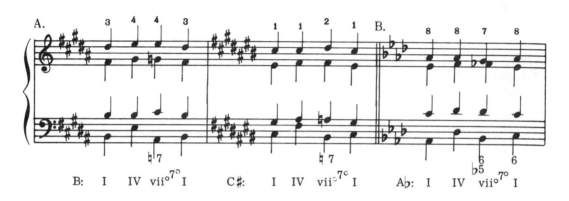

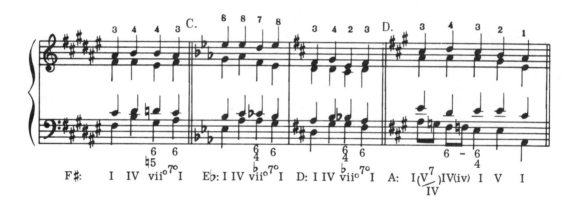

The Brahms Third Symphony provides an excellent example of the mixing of scale materials from major and minor. The key is F major; observe the use of the lowered sixth and third scale degrees.

Ex. 31.2.   Brahms, Third Symphony

A dramatic use of minor scale degrees in a major key appears in the slow movement of a Mozart Symphony. Included are the lowered 3rd, 6th, and 7th degrees, as well as the lowered 2nd in vii^{o7} of iv. The passage is firmly in B-flat major before and after the excursion into the parallel minor.

Ex. 31.3. Mozart, Symphony No. 40

II. Phrases with figured bass.

Observe the unique harmonic effect created by the use of the lowered sixth.

III. Melody harmonization.

Borrowed chords may be used to harmonize the lowered sixth scale degree in a melodic line; their more general function is as optional substitutes for their diatonic relatives.

The vii°⁷° (diminished) is more versatile than vii°⁷ (diminished-minor). It may appear in any inversion with any chord tone in the soprano.

Borrowed iv, ii°, and ii°⁷ may be used to add color to the harmonization; treating the lowered sixth as a chromatic passing tone will soften their effect. Scale degrees 4 and 2 are typical in the soprano.

IV⁷ is generally limited to an idiomatic use in third inversion with the sixth scale degree (ascending) in the soprano.

In this project the borrowed VI should be used only as an exaggerated deceptive cadence—with the tonic degree in the soprano.

Secondary dominants may also be used in these harmonizations.

Project 32

The Neapolitan Sixth; Augmented Triads

The so-called Neapolitan-sixth chord is a major supertonic whose root, and characteristic altera-tion, is the lowered second scale degree. The geographical designation has no technical significance, but is universally recognized and accepted. The qualifying "sixth" accurately suggests that the chord usually appears in first inversion. Since it contains the lowered sixth scale degree this chord is most readily employed in minor keys.

I. Typical settings.

The most common appearance of the Neapolitan sixth is in first inversion, with the fourth scale degree in the soprano. Like its close relatives, diatonic ii^{o6} and iv, it is preceded by tonic or sub-mediant triads and resolves to (or toward) some form of dominant harmony. The striking color of this chord is a result of the unusual root relationships—half step, tritone.

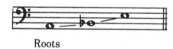

Roots

Play the progression i — N^6 — V — i in close structure in various minor keys. Experiment also with the optional additions to this progression indicated below. Learn to differentiate N^6 (major), ii^{o6} (diminished), and iv (minor).

3	(opt.) 5 3	4	(opt.) 3 3 3	2	1
i	i^6 or VI	N^6	i$^6_4$ or vii^{o7o}/v or III^{+6}	V	i

Illustrations:

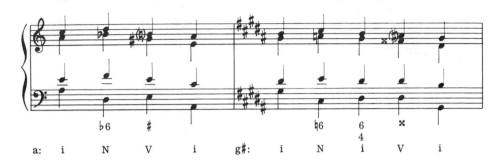

A concise illustration of the Neapolitan sixth is to be found at the conclusion of a well-known Chopin Prelude. The chord also appears in the introduction to Beethoven's "Moonlight" Sonata and is a significant part of the harmony throughout this work.

Ex. 32.1.   Chopin, Prelude No. 20

Ex. 32.2.   Beethoven, Piano Sonata, Op. 27, No. 2

The vocabulary of diatonic chords includes only one augmented triad, III$^+$ in minor. Augmented triads may also result from chromatic alterations. The most common of these are V$^+$ and I$^+$ in major keys, both created by chromatically raising the chord fifth—respectively, the raised second and fifth scale degrees. These altered tones have a strong tendency to resolve upward. The normal progression from an augmented triad is to a major triad with its root a fifth below. The third is sometimes doubled in the chord of resolution.

Other major triads (e.g., secondary dominants) may occasionally be similarly transformed by raising the chord fifth.

II. Phrases with figured bass.

The Neapolitan sixth and the augmented triad are distinctive and colorful sonorities, unmistakable in their aural effect. The abruptness of the root movement surrounding the Neapolitan sixth is lessened when the chord is not directly associated with i and V.

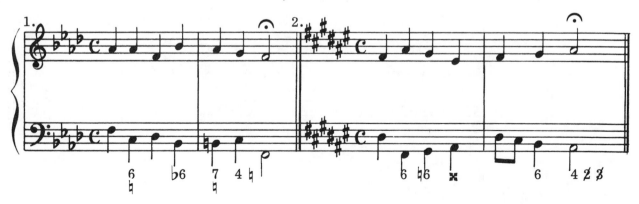

III. Melody harmonization.

Use N⁶ to harmonize the fourth, or lowered second, scale degree. The last two melodies provide opportunities to employ augmented tonic and dominant triads.

Chromatic Modulation

Modulations are classified as chromatic when they are effected through the use of chromatically altered chords or when there is melodic movement by chromatic half step in one or more of the parts. The chromaticism may be direct (in one part) or by cross relation (transferred between two parts). The modulating chord, often some form of dominant harmony in the new key, is not a diatonic chord common to both keys.

The technique of using chromaticism to effect a change of key is closely related to the secondary dominant concept. In the last five projects we have used chromatic and diatonic chords in a temporary (secondary) dominant-tonic relationship. When this transient tonic feeling is prolonged the new key center soon aurally supplants the original.

Compare the following harmonizations of two melodic passages.

The (a) harmonizations begin and end in the same key; each employs a secondary dominant. In the second versions, however, the implied tonics are reinforced (by an additional V — I) and thus establish a new key center.

I. Chromatic modulations with figured bass.

Play and analyze the following chromatic modulations. Observe first the modulation, identifying and comparing the two tonic centers. Secondly, observe the means by which the key change is accomplished; locate the chromatic voice-leading. The chromaticism directly precedes the new tonic and is most often in the bass part. Even in chromatic modulations, it is sometimes possible to locate a common chord; this analysis is not required since the chromaticism is a more definitive factor.

II. Secondary dominants and chromatic modulation.

The following problems illustrate the relationship between secondary dominants and chromatic modulation. Each phrase is to be completed in two ways:

1. In the original key—analyze the chromatic chord as a secondary dominant.

2. In a new key as suggested by the chromaticism—analyze as chromatic modulation.

These phrases can be completed with either half or authentic cadences using two or three additional chords in the suggested rhythms.

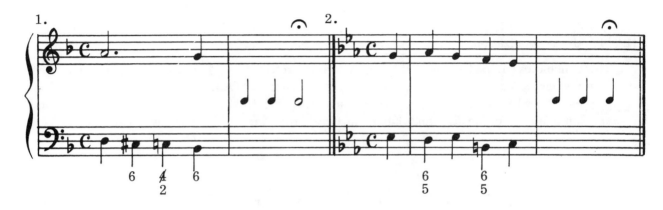

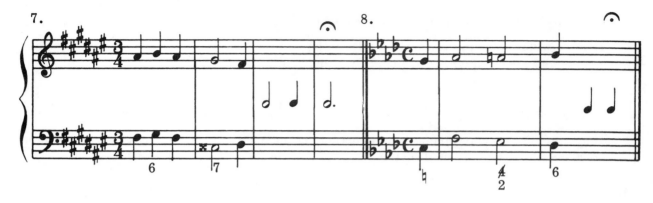

III. Melody harmonization.

These melodies can be harmonized in four ways: in each of the two indicated keys, and with modulations beginning in either key. For example, the first phrase can be set (1) in A♭ major, (2) in f minor, (3) with modulation from A♭ to f, and (4) with the modulation reversed. Use secondary dominants or chromatic modulations in two of the four harmonizations of each melody.

IV. Chromatic modulations to foreign keys.

The preceding chromatic modulations have utilized only near-related keys. Here are some more complex modulations which move to foreign keys. Play and analyze these. Aurally compare the two tonics; sing the chord roots. Root movement in fifths most strongly identifies a key center; chromatic modulations frequently involve root movement in seconds or thirds.

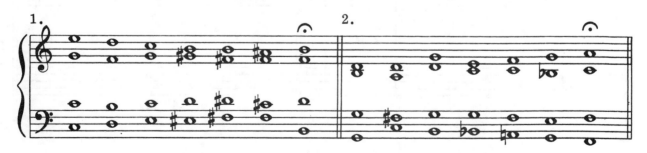

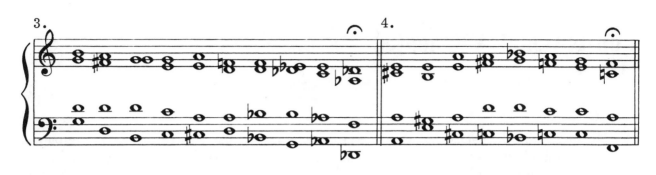

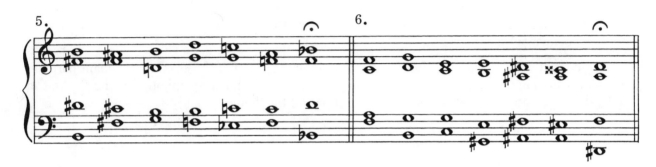

Project 34

Conventional Augmented-Sixth Chords

The interval of the augmented sixth (inverted diminished third) distinguishes this group of chords from all others in the traditional vocabulary, since all other triads and seventh chords, diatonic or chromatic, consist exclusively of superimposed major and minor thirds. Conventionally, the augmented sixth results from the combination of the lowered sixth scale degree in the bass with the raised fourth in any other part. The normal resolution of these active tones expands the augmented sixth to an octave on the dominant.

Augmented sixth chords are often used to heighten the effect of the ensuing dominant harmony. This is illustrated in the excerpt from the opening of Beethoven's Fifth Symphony. In the Brahms example, the augmented sixth chords are an integral part of the theme.

Ex. 34.1. Beethoven, Symphony No. 5, Op. 67

Ex. 34.2. Brahms, Symphony No. 1, Op. 68

I. The augmented sixth interval.

In each given key, play and resolve augmented sixths as follows:

1. Play the lowered sixth degree in the bass register. Note that this tone is diatonic in minor keys and chromatically lowered in major, but always lies a major third below the tonic.

2. Play the raised fourth scale degree in any higher register. This is an altered tone in both major and minor keys.

3. Play the resolution of the resultant augmented sixth to an octave on the dominant.

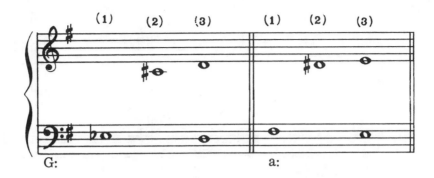

1. B major
2. C minor
3. F major
4. G minor
5. A-flat minor
6. D-sharp minor

7. E major
8. B-flat minor
9. G-flat major
10. C-sharp minor
11. A major
12. D minor

Conventional augmented sixth chords occur as alterations of IV⁶, ii₃⁴ and IV₅⁶. The three geographic names are universally employed and serve effectively as concise verbal symbols for these colorful musical effects. In major keys, the German-sixth sonority is sometimes more conveniently spelled as ii₃⁴; the chord may be identified (by its unique interval) as the chord of the doubly-augmented fourth.

(*Fig. Bass*)		*Major Keys*	*Minor Keys*
Italian sixth	$\overset{6}{\diagup}$	IV (♯4, ♭6)	iv (♯4)
French sixth	$\begin{matrix}6\\4\\3\end{matrix}$	ii⁷ (♯4, ♭6)	ii°⁷ (♯4)
German sixth	$\overset{6}{(♭)5}$	IV⁷ (♭3, ♯4, ♭6)	iv⁷ (♯4)
Doub.-aug. fourth	$\begin{matrix}6\\4\\3\end{matrix}$	ii⁷ (♯2, ♯4, ♭6)	- - - - -

Inasmuch as the presence of a diminished third in these chords tends to aurally obscure the root, it may be more practical to construct and identify them according to intervals present above the bass tone.

Italian:
Aug. 6th
Maj. 3rd

French:
Aug. 6th
Maj. 3rd
Aug. 4th

German:
Aug. 6th
Maj. 3rd
Perf. 5th

Doub.-aug.:
Aug. 6th
Maj. 3rd
D.-aug. 4th

II. Augmented sixth chords.

Play the following augmented sixth chords. Identify the key (the lowered sixth degree is in the bass) and the specific type of each chord. Sing the two tones that comprise the augmented sixth. Practice aural discrimination between chord types, noting especially the unique sound of the French sixth.

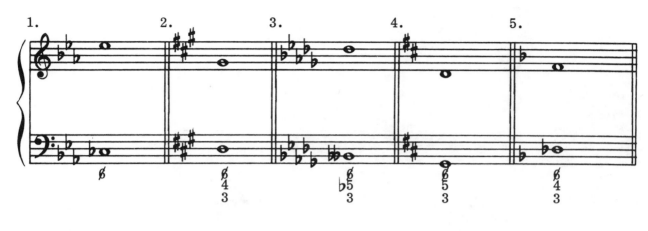

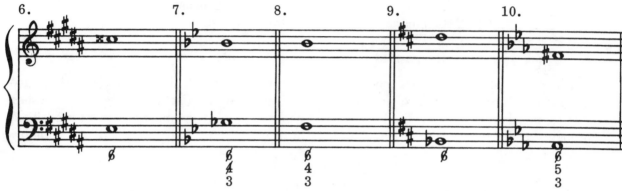

III. Typical settings.

Any of the three augmented sixth chords may harmonize the tonic scale degree. The French sixth also harmonizes the second degree, and the German sixth (or its enharmonic equivalent, the chord of the doubly-augmented fourth) harmonizes the minor third or raised second degree.

	1	1	1	7	1
A.	I	It.6	I$^{6}_{4}$	V	I
		—or—			
		F.6			
		—or—			
		G.6			

	3	2	3	2	1
B.	I	F.6	I$^{6}_{4}$	V	I

		(♯2)			
	3	3	3	2	1
C.	I	G.6	I$^{6}_{4}$	V	I

Illustrations:

IV. Phrases with figured bass.

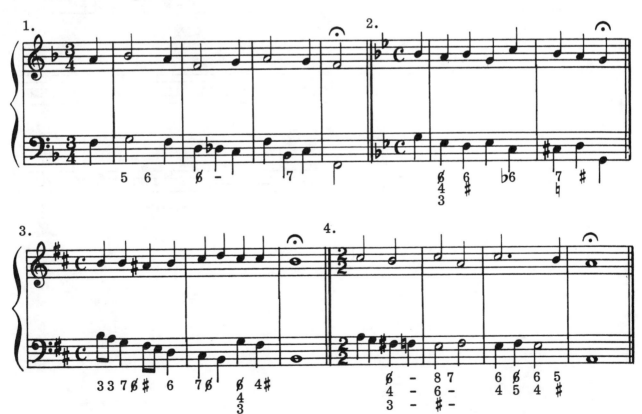

V. Melody harmonization.

Conventional augmented sixth chords harmonize diatonic scale degrees 1, 2, or 3. They may also accompany the raised fourth or raised second degrees, as illustrated in #1 below. When present, the arrows indicate where augmented sixth chords may be used. Scan each melody before harmonizing; use modulation when appropriate.

Review: Melody Harmonization
with Altered Chords

Altered chords extend harmonic resources in two principal ways: (1) by substituting for diatonic triads or sevenths in harmonizing diatonic melodies and (2) by accommodating, or generating, chromaticism in the melodic line. Melody harmonization, while potentially much more sophisticated, may still be accomplished through four general steps.

1. *Determine the key.* Unless the chromatic alterations appear in the soprano melody, the cadence formulas will have the same tonal implications as in diatonic harmonizations. Half cadences are frequently prepared by secondary dominants. Borrowed vii°⁷⁰ and VI increase the cadential options in major keys.

2. *Select appropriate triads or seventh chords.* The broadest spectrum of choices is available in this step. For a single melodic tone (e.g., the fourth scale degree) there may be as many as eighteen possible harmonizing chords! Related melodic conditions will, of course, restrict the number of options. The greatest variety of altered chords appear in a functional position twice-removed from the tonic center, i.e., normally progressing to the dominant. (See the summarizing diagram which follows.)

3. *Refine the bass line.* Secondary dominants most often occur with the characteristic alteration in the bass. Altered chords provide an opportunity to exploit direct, and extended, chromaticism in the bass; the descending tetrachord 8 − 5, for instance, may be completely filled-in chromatically.

4. *Add inner parts.* Continue to use nonharmonic tones and to prepare and resolve chord sevenths. The effect of an altered tone is often enhanced when it is delayed by suspension. Altered tones may also be used in a passing context in the inner parts.

The following diagram summarizes the chord vocabulary acquired to this point. This material should be compared with review projects 14 and 25.

Each chord group is subdivided into two columns containing the triad and seventh chord structures. The vertical divisions enumerate the chromatic equivalents of each diatonic chord: (1) secondary dominants; (2) borrowed chords [B.C.], Neapolitan sixth [N6], augmented triads; and (3) augmented sixth chords [It.6, G.6, F.6].

The arrows indicate the common progression, or general tendency, of each chord group, but do not exhaust all possibilities. The normal, systematic gravitation toward the tonic remains the same as with diatonic triads and sevenths.

This abstract diagram must be studied in the light of specific chord usage previously examined in greater detail. Remember that some of these altered chords are limited to either major or minor keys. In diatonic melodies altered chords generally harmonize the same scale degrees as their diatonic counterparts.

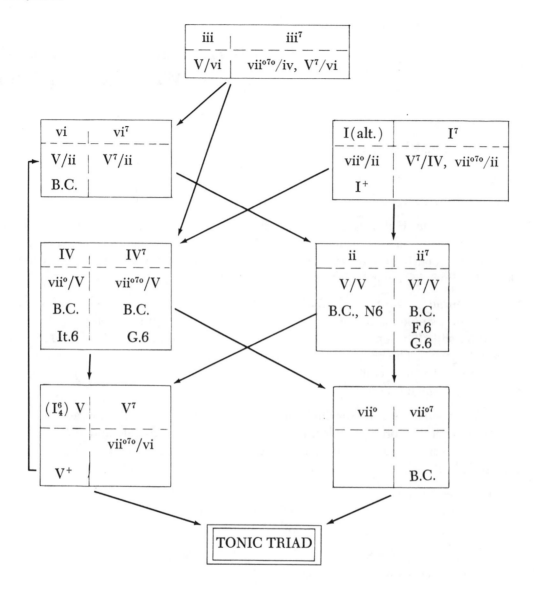

These chord relationships can be seen more clearly when translated into musical notation. The following diagram shows the diatonic and chromatic chords in the key of F major. Name each chord and illustrate a typical setting at the keyboard.

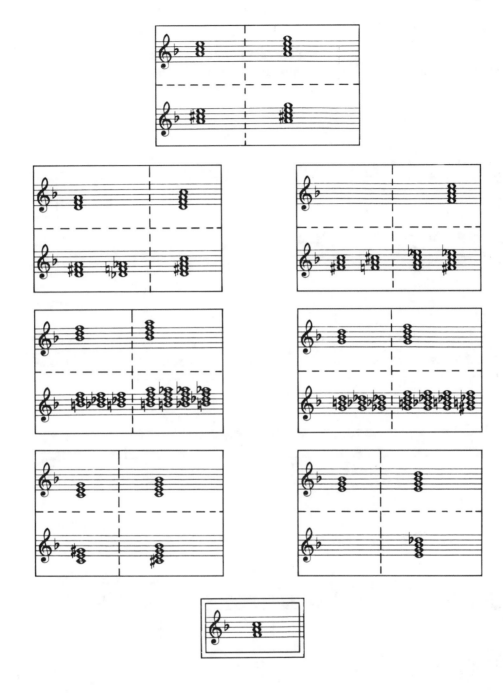

I. Chorales with unfigured bass.

Play these bass and soprano lines from chorale harmonizations by J. S. Bach. Then add the alto and tenor parts, including chromatic alterations as appropriate.

1. No. 118.

2. No. 146.

3. No. 313, last 3 phrases.

4. No. 279.

II. Chorale melodies.

   Altered tones are atypical in chorale melodies; the harmonizations, however, frequently employ altered tones, or extended chromaticism, in the bass. The following chorales offer numerous opportunities for the use of altered chords and chromatic modulation. Develop harmonizations by experimenting with various altered chords.

1.

2.

3.

III. Chromatic melodies.

Of the chromatic alterations studied thus far, the following are most likely to find melodic application.

Major keys:
- ♯1: Sec. dom. of ii
- ♯2: V⁺, A6
- ♭3: Sec. dom. of V
- ♯4: Sec. dom. of V, A6
- ♯5: Sec. dom. of vi, I⁺
- ♭6: B.C.
- ♭7: Sec. doms. of IV & ii

Minor keys:
- ♭2: Sec. dom. of iv, N6
- ♯3: Sec. dom. of iv
- ♯4: Sec. dom. of V, A6
- (♯6: Sec. dom. of V)

D major scale, with altered tones:

D natural minor scale, with altered tones:

Harmonize these chromatic melodies, using altered chords.

Unit IV
Advanced Chromaticism and Twentieth-Century Harmony

Project 36

Ninth Chords

Extending the projection of thirds beyond three- and four-tone chords results in the harmonic intervals of a ninth, eleventh, and thirteenth above the chord root.

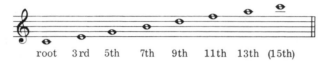

root   3rd   5th   7th   9th   11th   13th   (15th)

By superimposing major or minor ninths on various types of seventh chords several ninth chord types can be generated. The most important of these are the ninth chords built on major-minor sevenths: the major-minor-major ninth and the major-minor-minor ninth. These are the chords commonly and conveniently called major ninth (M9) and minor ninth (m9). Practice singing intervals of major and minor ninths, as well as the complete chords.

1 9   1 3 5 7 9 7 5 3 1   1 9   1 3 5 7 9 7 5 3 1

These two chords most often function as V⁹ or V⁹ of V, sometimes as V⁹ of IV. Other possible ninth chord types include the MMM⁹, as IV⁹ in major keys, and the mmM⁹ as iv⁹ in minor or ii⁹ in major.

We have observed that seventh chords often appear as transient, nonharmonic effects (e.g., passing tones, suspensions) rather than as independent chords. This is even more true in the case of ninths. Generally, if the interval of the ninth resolves before the chord changes it may be regarded as a nonharmonic tone.

The eleventh rarely, if ever, appears as a discrete chord, but rather is likely to be part of some nonharmonic effect. The *interval* of an eleventh is often found as a 4-3 suspension or as another temporary dissonance over a dominant pedal point.

The same is true of thirteenth chords, with one important exception. A chord consisting of the intervals M3, m7, and M or m13 above a root is quite common. The thirteenth is often a passing tone or suspension, but sometimes resolves by downward leap of a third, in which case it may analyzed as an independent chord. Observe how it is closely related to other dominant effects.

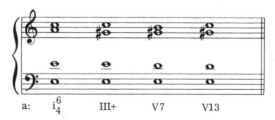

a: i⁶₄   III+   V7   V13

184

Ex. 36.1. Liszt, La Notte.

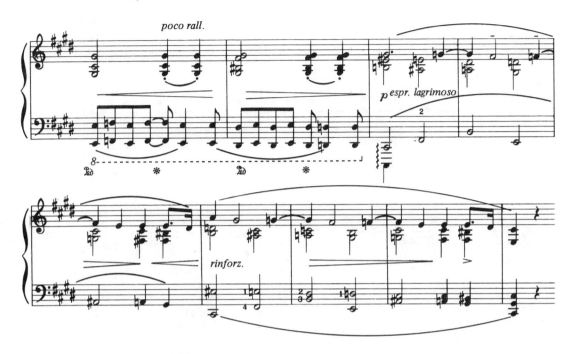

Ex. 36.2. Chopin, Ballade in F Major, Op. 38.

I. Typical settings.

A. $\dfrac{5 \quad\; 6 \quad\;\; 6 \quad\;\; 5}{\text{I} \quad \text{IV} \quad \text{V}^9 \quad \text{I}}$ C. $\dfrac{3 \quad\;\; 3 \quad\;\; 1}{\text{I} \quad \text{V}^{13} \quad \text{I}}$

B. $\dfrac{3 \quad\;\; 3 \quad\;\; 2 \quad\;\; 1}{\text{I} \quad \text{V}^9/\text{v} \quad \text{V} \quad \text{I}}$

Illustrations:

II. Phrases with figured bass.

Additional ninth chords include IV⁹ in major and minor keys, as well as ii⁹, V⁹/ɪᴠ and borrowed V⁹ (♭6) in major. Unless the chord change coincides with the resolution, ninths may be perceived as non-harmonic effects rather than as essential intervals. Observe the various ninth chord types and functions illustrated in these phrases.

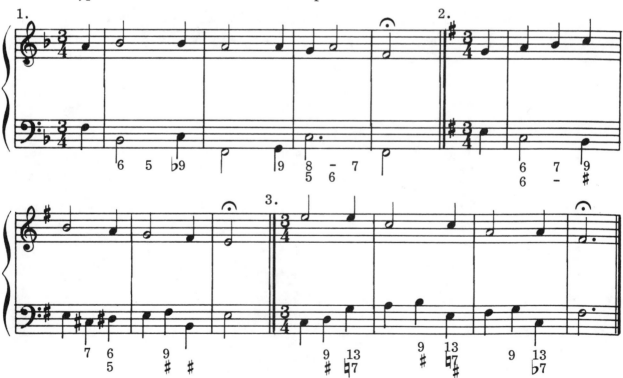

III. Melody harmonization.

V^9 and V^9/v (or ii^9 in major) most often harmonize scale degrees 6 and 3, respectively. The dominant thirteenth accompanies the third scale degree, usually at an authentic cadence.

Jazz Harmony

Ninth, eleventh, and thirteenth chords are idiomatic in jazz and related styles. The harmonic materials of jazz are too extensive and diverse to be treated thoroughly in this study, but it will be useful to consider some harmonic effects that are especially distinctive.[1]

Tonic Chords

Jazz pianists seldom make use of a simple, unadorned tonic triad. Common added notes are the intervals of a major sixth or major seventh above the root. Other possible additions include ninths, elevenths, or thirteenths.

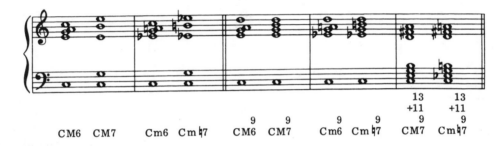

Dominant Chords

It is in the area of dominant harmony that the most striking chord structures are found. Chromatic alterations of the fifth of a dominant seventh chord are of particular interest. The chord fifth may be either raised or lowered by a half step. The raised fifth corresponds enharmonically to the minor thirteenth above the root; the lowered fifth corresponds to an augmented eleventh. Both resultant chords contain an interval of a diminished third—augmented sixth.

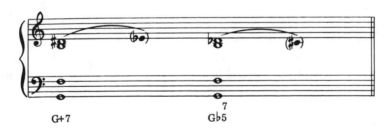

----

[1]In recent years a number of excellent books on jazz techniques have been published. Among their authors are Lee Burswold, Jerry Coker, Jerry Gray, Dan Haerle, Bert Konowitz, and John Mehegan. The student may also wish to investigate compositions and arrangements by Dave Brubeck, Bill Evans, and Oscar Peterson.

The author is also indebted to David Shumway for many of the ideas and exercises in this project.

Major or minor ninths can be added to these altered dominant sevenths. With the addition of a major ninth these chords include the six notes of a whole-tone scale.

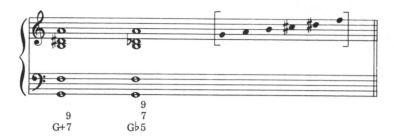

Another common jazz dominant is referred to, and spelled, as an augmented ninth. This interval is enharmonically identical to a minor tenth. The chord may have derived from the ambiguously pitched third of the so-called blues scale.

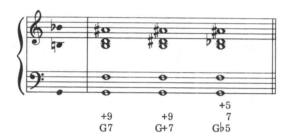

The preceding examples will suggest many other possibilities for complex harmonies generated by superimposed thirds and varied by chromatic alterations. It is possible to rationalize any tone of a chromatic scale as a chord tone.

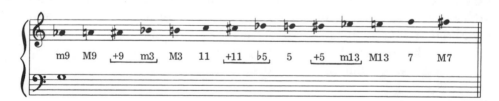

All of these dominant-function chords can be applied as secondary dominants. Diatonic seventh and ninth chords are also common in jazz harmonizations. For future reference, it may be observed here that many of these complex chords could be analyzed as superimposed triads.

Chord Voicings

Chords of the 7th, 9th, and 13th are commonly voiced in three parts with the third or seventh as the lowest note. Left-hand chord patterns for the progression ii − V − I may be voiced as follows.

F major

ii⁹ V¹³ I⁹   ii¹³ V⁹ I¹³

Chord Progressions

Two harmonic patterns are used extensively in jazz, ii − V − I (illustrated above) and the blues. The harmonic form of the blues is a universal language among jazz musicians. The underlying chord progressions are subjected to infinite variations and embellishments, but originate from very simple root movements. The standard 12-bar pattern is strongly characterized by movement to the sub-dominant in the fifth bar. The chord structures may be triads, 7ths, 9ths, or 13ths, and may include chromatic alterations.

Bar:	1	2	3	4	5	6	7	8	9	10	11	12
	I	IV	I	I	*IV*	IV	I	I	V	IV	I	I
									(or: vi	ii	V)	

Scales

Melodic tones which are most distinctive in the blues style are the minor third and seventh, and the raised fourth. These three tones, plus the diatonic fourth and fifth degrees, comprise the blues scale. The blues scale of the key may be used with tonic, dominant, and subdominant chords.

A systematic study of jazz encompasses many different scale possibilities, such as modal and synthetic forms. Common modal-harmonic associations are Dorian with ii, Mixolydian with V, and major with I. Chromatic tones are often added, as illustrated below.[1]

[1]See Project 41 for an explanation of modal scales.

Here are some of the other scale forms used in jazz. Observe the prominence of the lowered third and seventh and the raised fourth degrees.

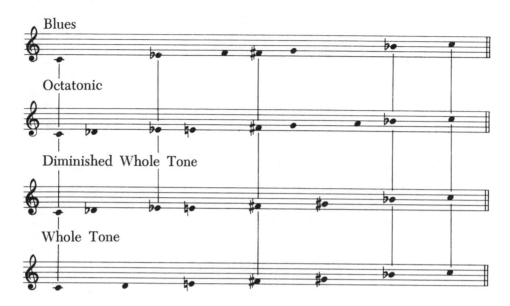

Chord Substitution

One further practice of jazz harmony may be mentioned. The general rule is that a chord may be replaced by another chord whose root is a tritone from the original. The substitute chord will usually be of the same type (e.g., m⁷, Mm⁷) as the chord it replaces. The tritone substitution is especially useful with dominant chords and is accomplished with minimal changing of other chord members. The substitute chords contain a re-spelled augmented sixth—d-flat, b-natural in the following examples.

Phrases in jazz style. Play and analyze; transpose to other keys.

1. The progression ii-v-I with jazz piano voicings. Rhythms should be performed as triplet patterns:

B. C major

C. F major

D. B♭ major

2. Fifth progressions: iii-vi-ii-V-I.

a. Sevenths

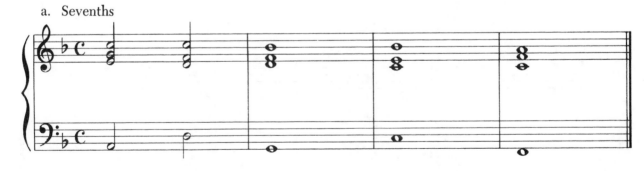

b. Ninths with alterations

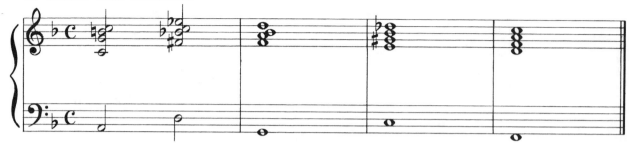

c. Extensions by repetition and substitution

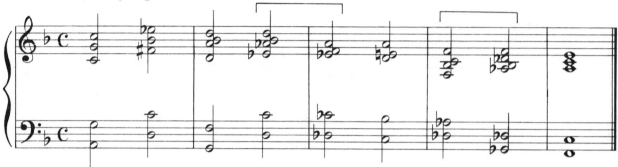

3. 12-bar blues accompaniment (bass tones added).

4. Other phrases.

A.

B.

C.

Project 38

Additional Uses of the Augmented Sixth

In Project 34 we examined the use of the augmented sixth interval in its most common applications. A thorough study of chromatic harmony requires consideration of other uses of this unique interval. These may be divided into three categories.

1. Inversion and/or respelling of conventional augmented sixth chords. These, and other augmented sixth chords, may be identified by a Roman numeral which reflects the spelling and an abbreviation (It., F., G.) indicating chord type.

The German sixth chord is enharmonically identical to a major-minor seventh. This identity becomes more apparent when the chord is inverted. By respelling (♭5 instead of ♯4) the chord may function as a secondary dominant of the Neapolitan triad.

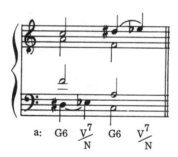

2. The augmented sixth formed between the lowered second degree and the leading-tone —vii°, vii°7, and V7 with the second scale degree chromatically lowered. These chords correspond to the dominant seventh with lowered fifth and the tritone dominant substitutes in the jazz vocabulary.

3. Finally, the augmented sixth is occasionally found at other positions in the scale—such as ♮4-♯2, ♭3-♯1, ♭7-♯5, ♭5-♮3. These situations occur only rarely. The analysis is, as always, dependent upon the prevailing tonality—the stronger the perception of key center, the clearer the identity of the harmonies.

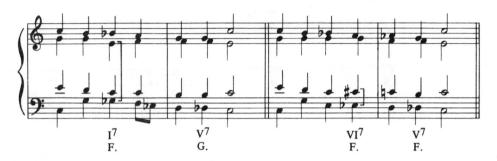

Because of its symmetrical structure, any French sixth chord may be respelled to form another French sixth. The two chords will always be a tritone apart.

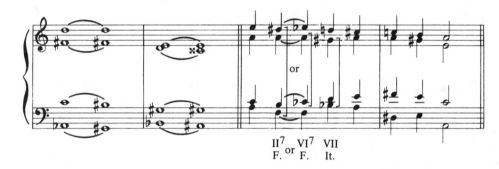

The augmented sixth interval also occurs in augmented dominant-type seventh chords. These chord structures do not conform to any of the three standard designations.

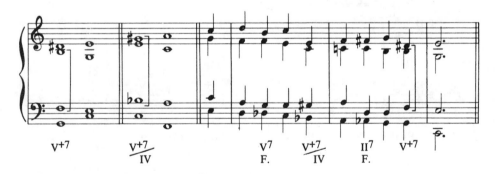

Augmented sixth chords of all types may be related to secondary dominant chords with one tone chromatically lowered. The conventional augmented sixth chords are derived from secondary dominants of V.

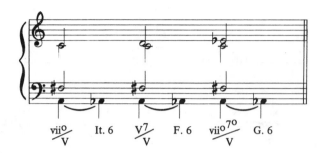

Other secondary dominant/augmented sixth relationships are shown below, all in the key of C major. This illustration includes only the French sixth type.

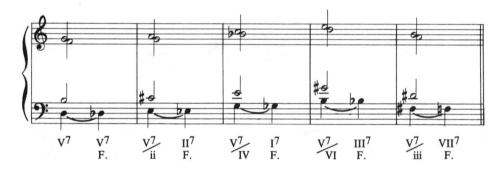

I. Examples from music literature; play and analyze.

Ex. 38.1. Chopin, Mazurka, Op. 63, No. 1

Ex. 38.2. Brahms, Sonata for Viola and Piano, Op. 120, No. 2

Ex. 38.3. Chopin, Mazurka, Op. 56, No. 3

Ex. 38.4. Chopin, Mazurka, Op. 7, No. 2

Ex. 38.5. Tchaikovsky, Swan Lake

Ex. 38.6. Carl A. Preyer, Variations on an Original Theme, Op. 32.

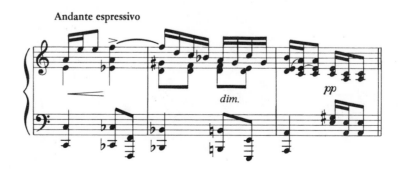

Ex. 38.7. Carl A. Preyer, Sonata No. 1, Op. 33.

Ex. 38.8. Carl A. Preyer, Scherzo in C Minor.

Ex. 38.9. Brahms, Symphony No. 2 (string parts, reduced)

II. Unconventional augmented-sixth chords.

   Play and analyze in the keys indicated. Identify and sing the augmented sixth, or diminished third, in each chord.

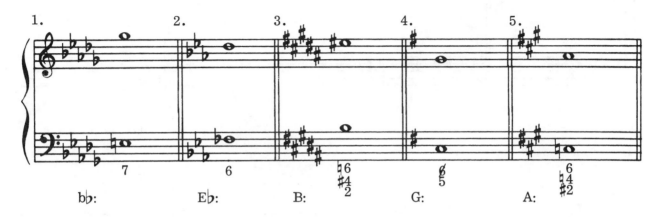

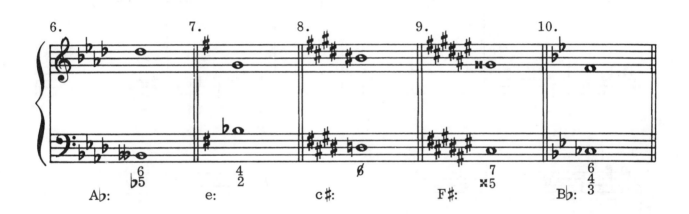

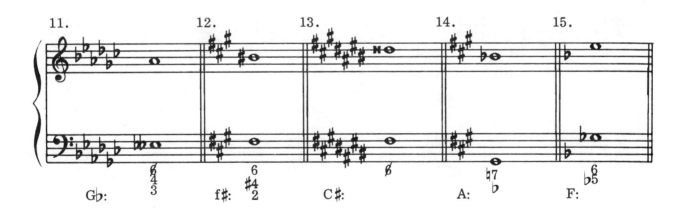

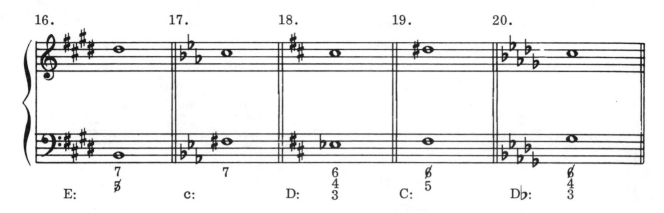

III. Phrases with figured bass.

IV. Melody harmonization.

Various augmented-sixth chords may harmonize the chromatic tones ♯4 or ♭2 in any key, as well as ♯2 and ♭6 in major. In these harmonizations, consider using the lowered second degree in any viiº, viiº⁷º, or V⁷. Arrows suggest possible locations for augmented sixths in the first four melodies.

Enharmonic Modulation (I)

This is the third of the three traditional modulatory techniques, the other two being diatonic modulation (Projects 16 and 17) and chromatic modulation (Project 33). Enharmonic modulation is similar to diatonic modulation in that both exploit the potential of a chord to function in more than one key. In the enharmonic technique, however, this duality is derived through the re-spelling, actual or implied, of one or more tones. Enharmonic modulations may move between near-related or remote keys. In this project we will examine the enharmonic identity of the intervals of the augmented sixth and the minor seventh.

The German sixth chord and the major-minor seventh are enharmonically identical; that is, they have the same sound but different spellings. We have seen that both of these chords have a variety of functions. We can now add the possibility of exploiting their enharmonic potential by exchanging functions between the two chords. Some possibilities are illustrated below—one chord sound with six possible functions in twelve major and minor keys.

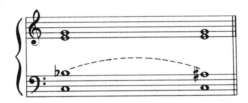

keys	functions		keys	functions
F-f	V⁷		E-e	IV⁷, G.
C-c	V⁷/IV		B-b	VII⁷, G.
B-b	V⁷/V		G-g	II, G.

I. Examples from music literature. Play and analyze.

A dramatic use of enharmonic relationships appears in the last movement of Brahms' First Symphony. The key center alternates between E minor and C major, with the latter finally prevailing as the return to the principal theme begins (mm. 11-12 of the excerpt). The movement from E minor to C major hinges on the F major triad—N becomes IV. The reverse modulation, C to E, relies on the enharmonic potential of the note, b♭ — a♯ — V⁷/IV becomes Aug. 6th.

Ex. 39.1. Brahms, Symphony No. 1, Op. 68

The identity of the major-minor seventh and German sixth chords was observed in the preceding project, when the chord was introduced as a secondary dominant of the Neapolitan triad. Modulation may result from a prolongation of the Neapolitan key center. This passage alternates between keys a half step apart. The German sixth $(f\flat, a\flat, c\flat, d)$ becomes V^7 $(e, g\sharp, b, d)$; the returning modulation is accomplished by exchanging tonic for Neapolitan function $(a, c\sharp, e$ becomes $b\flat\flat, d\flat, f\flat)$.

Ex. 39.2. Schubert, Moment Musicale, Op. 94, No. 6

The Italian sixth is the inharmonic equivalent of an incomplete major-minor seventh. There are two consecutive modulations in the next example, each apparently moving the key center up a half step. The continuation of this passage (not shown), however, is in B minor—the Italian sixth becoming V^7/v.

Ex. 39.3. Chopin, Sonata, Op. 58

The augmented sixth chord may interchange with other secondary dominants, for instance V^7/iv. In this situation the two keys are near-related.

Ex. 39.4. Bach, Chorale No. 300

These modulations operate equally well in reverse—with the major-minor seventh becoming the German sixth. It is usually impractical to show enharmonic spellings in a musical score. The most readily perceived spelling is used, generally that which conforms to the resolution of the tones. Chord repetition affords an opportunity to show both spellings.

Ex. 39.5. Chopin, Sonata, Op. 35

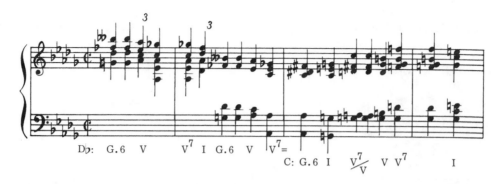

Db: G.6   V   V⁷ I G.6 V |V⁷=

C: G.6 I   V⁷/V   V V⁷   I

Applying this technique in sequence results in modulations in descending half steps.

Ex. 39.6. Chopin, Sonata, Op. 4

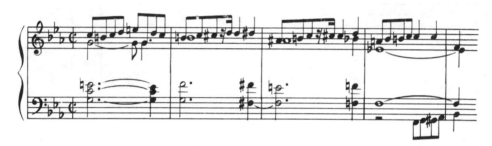

In Ex. 39.7 a secondary dominant becomes a German sixth; the keys are near-related.

Ex. 39.7. Beethoven, Sonata, Op. 79

II. Chords with enharmonic spellings.

Play, analyze, and resolve each chord in the indicated key. Extend the resolutions through an authentic cadence to clearly establish the key center.

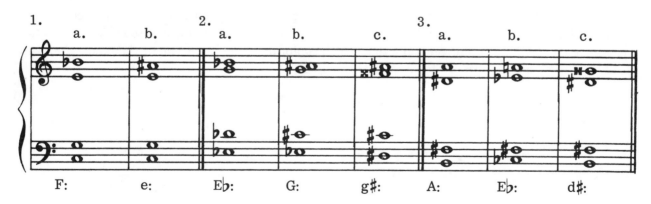

1.   a.   b.   2. a.   b.   c.   3. a.   b.   c.

F: e: Eb: G: g#:   A: Eb: d#:

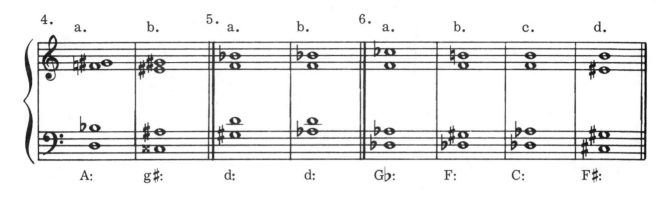

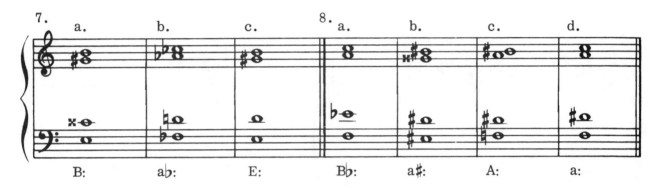

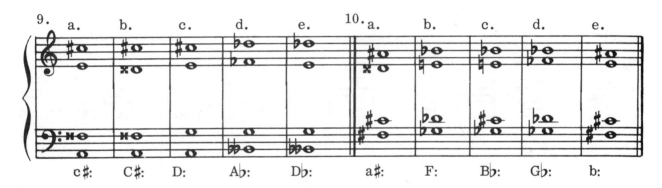

III. Phrases with unfigured bass.

   Add inner parts to create appropriate harmonies. Each phrase should include an enharmonic modulation. The arrows indicate points at which the enharmonic exchange may occur.

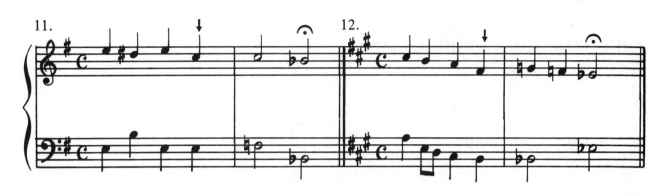

Project 40

Enharmonic Modulation (II)

The chameleon-like quality of the diminished-seventh chord derives from its symmetrical structure. The four tones are spaced equi-distantly, dividing an octave into four segments of three semitones each.[1] The chord sounds the same in all inversions; consequently, any of the four tones may function as the chord root.

Considered enharmonically, there are only three mutually exclusive diminished-seventh chords. These are illustrated below with some of their enharmonic spellings.

The most common functions of the diminished-seventh chord are

Major keys:	Minor keys:
1. vii⁰⁷° (B.C.)	1. vii⁰⁷°
2. vii⁰⁷°/v	2. vii⁰⁷°/v
3. vii⁰⁷°/ii	3. vii⁰⁷°ᵢᵥ

All three of the diminished-seventh chords can function in any given key. Study the following settings in C major and F-sharp minor.

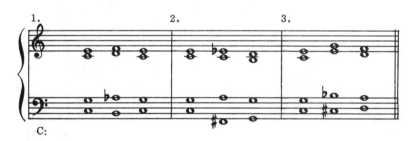

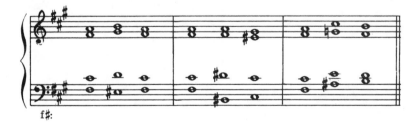

---

[1]The other sonorities which equally divide an octave are the tritone, augmented triad, and the whole-tone scale. See Appendix 1.

Any one of the diminished-seventh chords can function in all keys. This illustration uses the chord, b–d–f–a♭, with several enharmonic spellings. Twelve of the thirty conventional keys are included.

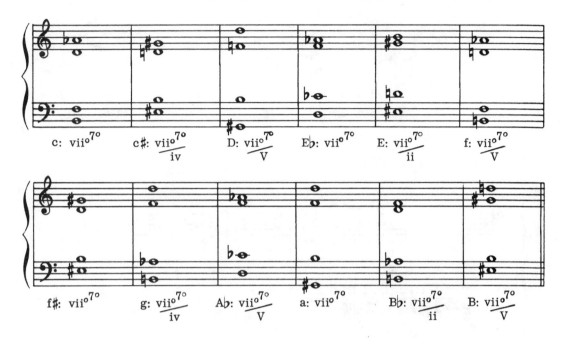

The preceding examples serve to demonstrate the broad principle which governs enharmonic modulation through the diminished seventh: *any diminished-seventh chord can function in any key.*

This versatility makes the diminished seventh chord extremely useful in modulations. The first two examples below are two passages from the same work that modulate through enharmonic exchange of the diminished seventh. The first example moves from B-flat major to F-sharp minor—the chord b-d-f-a♭ becomes e♯-g♯-b-d. The second passage modulates down a half step, from B major to B-flat minor. The pivot chord is the diminished seventh b♯-d♯-f♯-a, enharmonically a-c-e♭-b♭.

Ex. 40.1. Schubert, Piano in B♭ major, Op. posth.

Ex. 40.2. Schubert, op. cit.

Ex. 40.3. Three Piano Pieces, No. 2 "Allegretto"

Ex. 40.4. Chopin, Mazurka, Op. 7, No. 4.

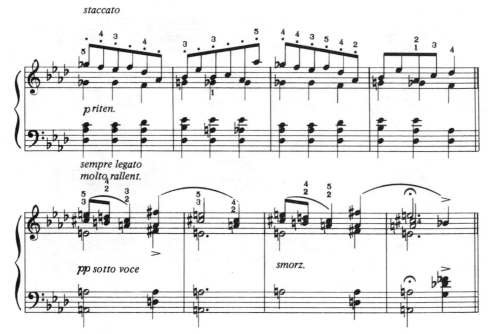

Ex. 40.5. Chopin, Mazurka, Op. 17, No. 3.

Lowering any member of a diminished-seventh chord by a semitone results in a major-minor seventh chord. The resulting major-minor seventh is, of course, enharmonically identical to an augmented sixth.

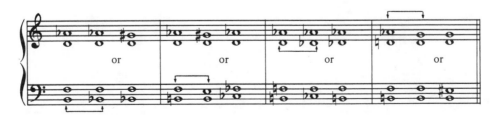

Modulations may utilize this effect, thus including the enharmonic potentials of both the augmented sixth and the diminished seventh.

There are three augmented-sixth chords in Example 6, suggested the keys of C minor, A-flat minor, and F minor. These chords are linked by a common diminished-seventh chord, b, d, f, a♭, which is transformed by chromatically lowering one of its members—f to f♭ and d to d♭.

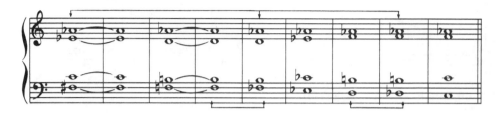

Ex. 40.6.   Tchaikovsky, Swan Lake

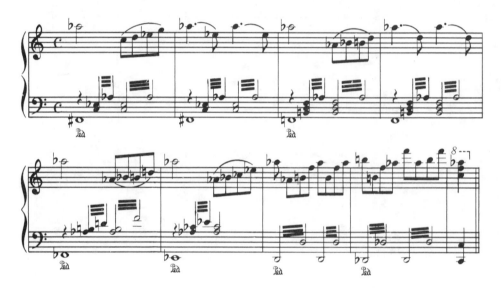

Ex. 40.7.   Chopin, Mazurka, Op. 17, No. 4.

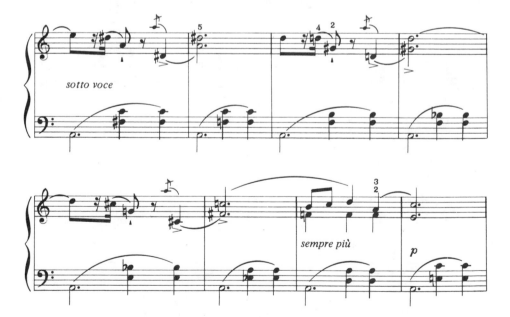

I. Resolving diminished-seventh chords.

Play, analyze, and resolve each chord in the indicated key. Recall that the diminished-seventh chord normally resolves with stepwise motion in all parts. Inverted diminished-seventh chords usually move to inverted triads.

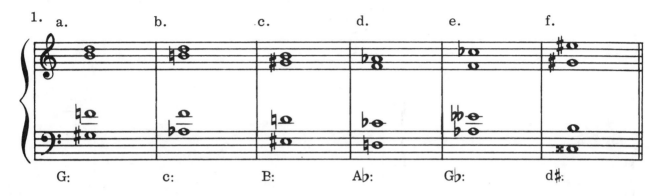

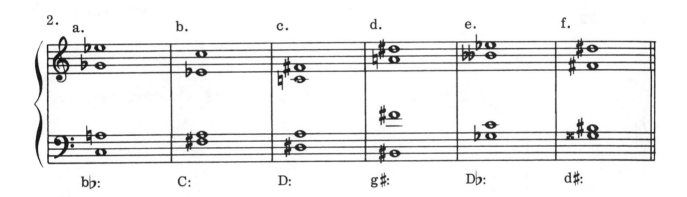

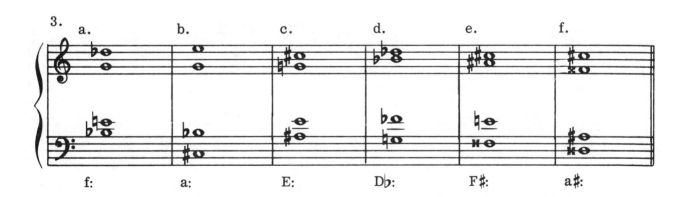

II. Phrases with unfigured bass.

These are arranged in three sets, each utilizing one of the three basic diminished sevenths. Carefully analyze the enharmonic exchange at each ↓

III. Phrases with figured bass.

Arrows indicate the points of enharmonic exchange

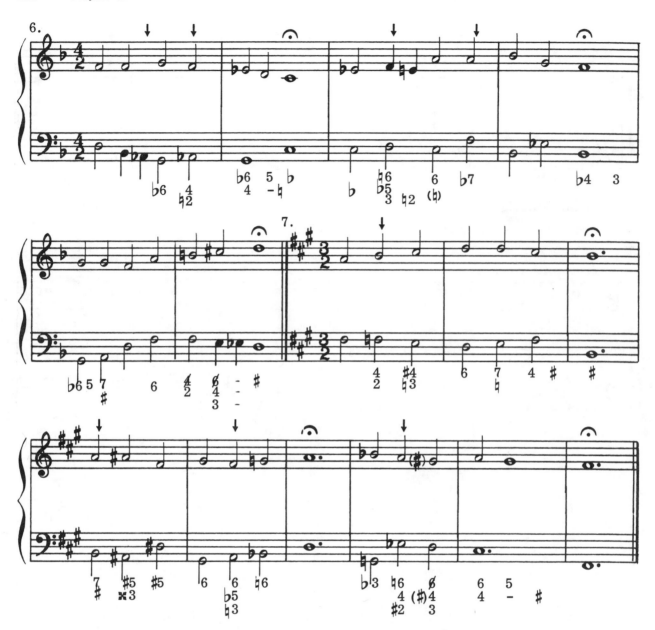

Harmonic Sequence

Sequence, the direct recurrence of a musical idea on a different pitch level, has traditionally been one of the most vital organizing factors in music. In the first unit of this book simple, tonal sequences were included as learning aids to demonstrate chord relationships and voice leading. In this project we will examine harmonic sequences in another context—as a means of organizing passages which may otherwise seem inexplicable within the limits of conventional analysis. Before proceeding to these more complex situations it will be useful to review the more simple types of sequences.

1. Tonal sequences.

Traditional tonality has a basic sequential implication—root movement in descending fifths.

Secondary dominants offer an additional resource for sequential development within a key.

2. Modulating sequences.

The preceding illustration suggests modulation, and might be so perceived depending on tempo and harmonic rhythm. When the transient key centers are not near-related, and when more than two chords are used in the sequence, modulation is more strongly implied. Indeed, conventional practice does not provide an alternative to the analysis of these passages as a series of brief, transitory modulations.

Ex. 41.1. Chopin, Mazurka, Op. 56, No. 1

The sequence of V-I progressions creates a rapid change of key centers in the following passage. Note that each temporary tonic is enharmonically a Neapolitan triad in the subsequent key.

Ex. 41.2. Chopin, Mazurka, Op. 59, No. 1

The following example shows another sequential modulation, but this time with an additional chord inserted between the tonic of the old key and the dominant of the new. The unique color in this progression results from lowering the root of the diminished seventh to create a new dominant seventh. The melody line, with chromatic passing tones, is an ascending chromatic scale. An analysis by root and chord type, beginning with the pick-up to m. 3, would appear as follows:

$$\boxed{A^7 \quad D \quad c\#^{o7o}} \quad \begin{matrix} \text{Up} \\ \text{mi. 3} \end{matrix} \quad \boxed{C^7 \quad F \quad e^{o7o} \quad \text{etc.}}$$

Ex. 41.3. Chopin, Mazurka, Op. 50, No. 3

3. Sequences including nonfunctional relationships.

Some harmonic relationships cannot be readily explained by conventional analysis. The usual procedure of identifying harmonic function by chord numerals is inadequate to account for root relationships that may lie outside the diatonic system. In such situations, the sequence itself may be the primary organizing factor. The analysis is directed to the sequential pattern rather than to the functional identity of each chord.[1]

The famous sequence from the opening of Scheherazade (reduced from the orchestral score) manifests a similar series of dominant-tonic relationships separated by other progressions unified primarily by common tones. The chromatic bass line is an important unifying factor. Observe also the tritone root relationships and the acceleration of the sequence. While this passage could be regarded as a series of rapid modulations, one chord in the series can not be accounted for by conventional numeral analysis.

| C♯ | E⁷ | B♭⁷ | Up M. 2 | E♭ | G♭⁷ | C⁷ | Up M. 2 | F | A♭⁷ | D⁷ | etc. |

Ex. 41.4. Rimsky-Korsakov, Scheherazade

----

[1]For an insightful discussion of this topic, see: John Pozdro, "Resources for the Interpretation of Non-functional Tertian Harmonic Progression" in The American Music Teacher, September-October, 1982.

I. Examples from music literature.

The following sequential passages all include nonfunctional harmonic relationships. Play and analyze.

Ex. 41.5. Wagner, Tristan & Isolde.

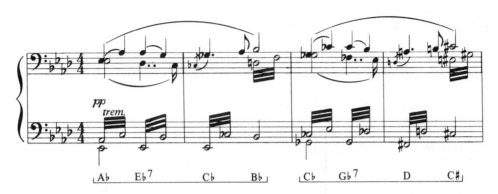

Ex. 41.6. Mozart, Fantasia in C Minor

Ex. 41.7. Chopin, Mazurka, Op. 17, No. 4

G⁷   e   F#⁷ d#   F⁷ d   E⁷

Ex. 41.8. Chopin, Mazurka, Op. 68, No. 4

e°⁷ E♭⁷   f#°⁷   D⁷   g#°⁷   D♭⁷
        (d#°⁷)   (c×°⁷)

Ex. 41.9. Wagner, Siegfried

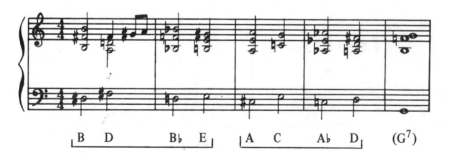

B D   B♭ E   A C A♭ D   (G⁷)

Ex. 41.10. Wagner, Parsifal

Ex. 41.11. Wagner, Siegfried

Ex. 41.12. Strauss, Der Rosenkavalier, Act I.

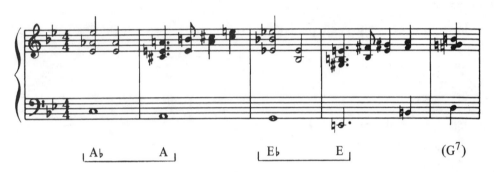

Copyright 1909, 1911, 1912 by Adolph Furstner. Renewed 1938, 1940. Copyright and renewal assigned to Boosey & Hawkes, Inc. Reprinted by permission.

Ex. 41.13. Strauss, Der Rosenkavalier, Act III.

Copyright 1909, 1911, 1912 by Adolph Furstner. Renewed 1938, 1940. Copyright and renewal assigned to Boosey & Hawkes, Inc. Reprinted by permission.

Ex. 41.14. Puccini, Madame Butterfly, Act II

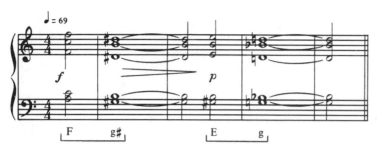

Copyright © 1954 by G. Ricordi & Co. Used by permission of Associated
Music Publishers, Inc.

II. Harmonic sequences.

Analyze the sequence, play each passage, and continue through one or two additional statements.

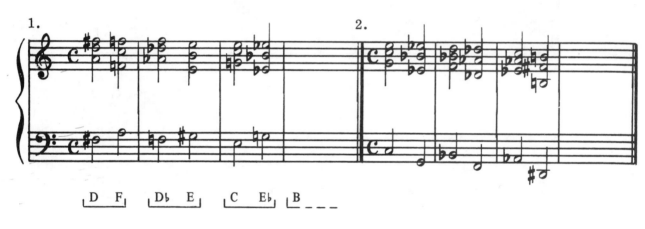

III. Sequences in keyboard style.

Improvise a continuation of each passage by extending the established sequence through two or more additional statements.

3.

4.

The chord vocabulary which was developed through the first 40 projects of this book enables us to assign a functional analysis to a large number of possible chords within a key. About 50 chords, more or less, can be functionally identified by their relationship to a given tonal center. While this number is great, it still leaves many possibilities unaccounted for. Here, for instance, are some chords which would be very difficult to explain within the context of C major.

Moreover, functional analysis is dependent on the recognition of a key center, or tonic, to which other chords can be related. In passages where the key center is obscure or absent the classification of chords by their tonal role is not possible.

This project has demonstrated how certain nonfunctional passages may be justified by harmonic sequence. Such unusual progressions also occur singularly, without sequential reiteration. The two examples below are included as samples of harmonic relationships which strain the limits of tonality. Analyze first by root and chord type, and then determine which of the chords can be functionally identified.

Ex. 41.15. Wagner, Parsifal, Act III.

Ex. 41.16. Strauss, Salome

Copyright 1905 by Adolph Furstner. Renewed 1933. Copyright and renewal assigned to Boosey & Hawkes, Inc. Reprinted by permission.

Modal Harmony

Diatonic scales may be defined as those which use seven different tones arranged consecutively as whole steps and half steps and which contain one tritone and two minor seconds. There are seven such scales, illustrated here using d as the tonic, or "final." The two half steps in each scale are marked.

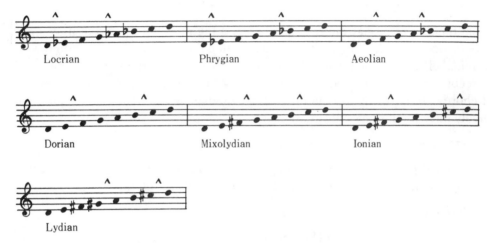

The *material* of the Ionian mode is identical to that of a major scale; the same relationship occurs between Aeolian mode and natural minor. Locrian mode is seldom used, especially in a harmonic context, because of its diminished tonic triad.

Our system of equal temperament allows for the transposition of any mode to any pitch level. Relative to our tonally-conditioned perception the six common church modes seem to divide into two general groups: three scales having major tonic triads and three having minor tonics. The Lydian, Mixolydian, Dorian, and Phrygian modes each have one distinctive scale degree. Transposition may be accomplished by modifying major or minor key signatures to accommodate the modal material.

	Mode	*Characteristic*	*Signature*
Modes with	Ionian	- - same as major - -	
major tonic:	Lydian	♯4	one more sharp
	Mixolydian	♭7	one more flat
Modes with	Aeolian	- - same as minor - -	
minor tonic:	Dorian	♯6	one more sharp
	Phrygian	♭2	one more flat

[1]Historically the church modes developed as a *melodic* (monophonic, later polyphonic) syntax. This study relates to the more recent interest in the modes as an enrichment of diatonic tonality in a harmonic texture.

Modal harmony is distinguished from conventional tonal harmony in two principal ways: (1) triad types and (2) root movement.

Major and minor triads occur at various points in modal scales. Prominent use of chords containing the subtonic degree often identifies modal harmony. The diminished triad (one per mode) is generally avoided: the tritone seems to be inappropriate to the "pure" modal effect. Inversions occur somewhat less frequently in modal harmonizations. In each of the four modes using material other than that of major or natural minor, there are two triads (one major, one minor) containing the characteristic scale degree. These triads are especially useful in establishing the modal color.

Lydian (♯4): II, vii	Dorian (♯6): ii, IV
Mixolydian (♭7): v, VII	Phrygian (♭2): II, vii

Traditional tonality is most strongly generated by a high frequency of root movement in descending fifths; progressions in seconds (most often ascending) and thirds (most often descending) occur less often. A modal effect may be created by reversing these proportions; the result is a much higher incidence of second and third relationships, ascending or descending. Seventh chords and chromatically altered chords are typically associated with root movement in fifths. Consequently, these sonorities are relatively infrequent in modal situations.

I. Modal progressions.

Play these modal progressions on various pitch levels. All triads may be played in root position. Develop soprano melodies which generally move in contrary motion to the bass.

A. The characteristic triads.

Lydian: I — II — vii — I — vii — II — I
Mixolydian: I — v — VII — I — VII — v — I
Dorian: i — ii — IV — i — IV — ii — i
Phrygian: i — II — vii — i — vii — II — i

B. Other progressions emphasizing second and third relationships. Analyze by chord type and function, e.g., minor iv, major III, etc. (The Roman numerals do not designate chord types in these examples.)

Ionian, Dorian, Phrygian: I — IV — III — II — I — II — III — IV — I
Lydian, Mixolydian, Aeolian: I — V — VI — VII — I — VII — VI — V — I
Dorian, Lydian, Aeolian: I — VII — V — III — I — III — V — VII — I
Ionian, Phrygian, Mixolydian: I — II — IV — VI — I — VI — IV — II — I

Illustrations:

A.

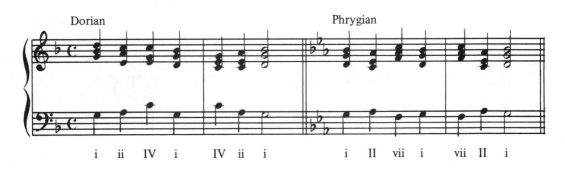

Dorian   Phrygian

i ii IV i IV ii i   i II vii i vii II i

B.

or or

I IV III II I II III IV I

or or

I V VI VII I VII VI V I

or or

I VII V III I III V VII I

or or

I II IV VI I VI IV II I

II. Phrases with figured bass.

III. Melody and accompaniment.

First identify the mode and analyze the harmony. Then play the passage and improvise a continuation or completion in the same style.

1.

2.

3.

4.

5.

Carol Bowman

The Pentatonic Scale

Many melodies which have a modal implication actually employ fewer than the seven tones available in a diatonic mode. The pentatonic (five-note) scale is essentially defined by the absence of tritones and minor seconds. Innumerable folk songs are set in this simple vocabulary.

There are five potential pentatonic "modes"; their differences, however, are minimal due to their uniform avoidance of dissonant color.

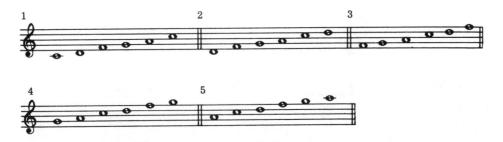

For the purpose of this study, these pentatonic scales may be regarded as incomplete diatonic scales. Each results from the omission of two diatonic tones, one from each tetrachord. Their modal implication is ambiguous; thus a pentatonic melody may be harmonized in any of three diatonic modes.

Pentatonic Mode	Complementary Diatonic Modes
1	Dorian, Ionian, Mixolydian
2	Phrygian, Dorian, Aeolian
3	Mixolydian, Lydian, Ionian
4	Aeolian, Mixolydian, Dorian
5	Locrian, Aeolian, Phrygian

It is interesting to observe that the Aeolian, Dorian, and Mixolydian modes exhibit the closest affinity to the pentatonic vocabulary. These lie at the center of the modal system, and the greatest number of folk remedies are set in one of these three modes.

IV. Pentatonic folk melodies for harmonization at the keyboard.

These simple melodies have been selected because of their adaptability to various harmonic settings. Determine the complementary diatonic modes for each melody and experiment with different harmonizations. Use either four-part or melody and accompaniment texture.

1. Little David (Mode 3)

2. Lonesome Road (Mode 3, incomplete)

3. The Trees They Do Grow High (Mode 4)

4. Come All Ye Fair and Tender Maidens (Mode 4)

5. Amazing Grace (Mode 3)

Parallel Harmony; The Whole-Tone Scale

The impressionistic style of composition contributed several innovations to harmonic practice. There are a number of techniques which might be cited as characteristics of this style such as the use of the pentatonic scale, incomplete triads, modal effects, prolonged pedal points, very slow harmonic rhythm, etc. Two features, however, stand out as particularly significant and idiomatic to impressionism. These are the primary topics of this project: (1) the whole-tone scale and (2) parallel harmony.

The Whole-Tone Scale

The study of nonfunctional, nontertian, or otherwise unconventional sonorities may be facilitated by a systematic analysis of their intervallic content. This type of analysis is accomplished by grouping all possible intervals into six basic categories. Each category represents an interval and its inversion as well as any enharmonic equivalent or octave displacement. For instance, the minor third group includes also the major sixth, augmented second, etc.[1] Arranged progressively from "consonant" to "dissonant," the six basic interval categories are: (1) perfect fourth—perfect fifth, (2) major third—minor sixth, (3) minor third—major sixth, (4) major second—minor seventh, (5) minor second—major seventh, and (6) tritone (augmented fourth or diminished fifth).

The whole-tone scale is comprised of six consecutive whole steps per octave. It contains only three of the six basic intervals: major thirds (6), major seconds (6), and tritones (3). The whole-tone scale differs most significantly from diatonic scales by its exclusion of perfect intervals. It does, however, have some important modal features: the ♯4 and ♭7 of Lydian and Mixolydian modes.

All triads (built in thirds) in this scale are augmented. The six-note, whole-tone scale can be harmonized with its two component augmented triads.

Four-note combinations derived from the whole-tone scale merit special study. There are only three of these; they are not without conventional precedent, but are often uniquely employed in an impressionistic context. These are exemplified below in three ways:

1. An example of the basic 4-note combination—various spellings, transpositions, and inversions could be applied.

2. Examples of the conventional scoring of these chords—as ninths, thirteenths, French sixths, etc.

3. Five examples of impressionistic scoring, extracted and reduced from piano works by Debussy.

---

[1]This analytical technique is introduced by Howard Hanson in *Harmonic Materials of Modern Music*, Appleton-Century-Crofts, Inc., 1960. Allen Forte has extended this principle in *The Structure of Atonal Music*, Yale University Press, 1973. Forte's six "interval classes" are numbered consecutively from the smallest, one semitone, to the largest, six semitones.

A. Major-ninth type, containing 3 major seconds.

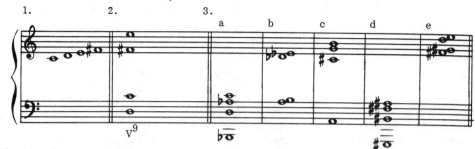

B. Minor-thirteenth type, containing 3 major thirds.

C. French-sixth type, containing 2 tritones.

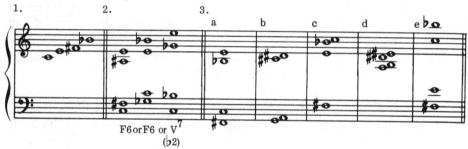

I. Whole-tone chords.

Play the following chords and sing each of the four tones in your vocal range. Classify each chord according to the three types illustrated above.

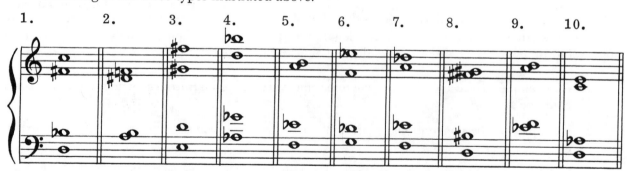

Parallel Harmony

The technique of using a series of chords (or intervals) in a parallel series, either as thickened melody or as accompaniment, is sometimes referred to as "planing." In such passages the chords are exploited as pure color, rather than as functional components of a particular key. The parallelism may be exact (same chord and inversion throughout) or varied (different chord types or inversions, sometimes conforming to a key).

The first two examples below illustrate the use of the whole-tone scale.

Ex. 43.1. Debussy, Voiles

Copyright 1910 Durand et Cie. Used by permission of the publisher Theodore Presser Company, Sole Representative U.S.A.

Ex. 43.2. Debussy, L'isle joyeuse

Additional excerpts illustrate the planing of major triads, augmented triads, major-minor sevenths, and major ninths.

Ex. 43.3. Debussy, Les sons et les parfums tournent dans l'air du soir

Copyright 1910 Durand et Cie. Used by permission of the publisher Theodore Presser Company, Sole Representative U.S.A.

Ex. 43.4. Debussy, Ce qu'a vu le vent d'ouest

Copyright 1910 Durand et Cie. Used by permission of the publisher Theodore Presser Company, Sole Representative U.S.A.

Ex. 43.5. Debussy, Nuages

Copyright 1923 Societe Des Editions Jobert. Used by permission of the publisher Theodore Presser Company, Sole Representative U.S.A.

The planing technique has found application in other styles as well. Here are two examples from well known operas.

Ex. 43.6. Puccini, Madame Butterfly, Act I.

Copyright © 1954 by G. Ricordi & Co. Used by permission of Associated Music Publishers, Inc.

Ex. 43.7. Strauss, Elektra (voice part omitted)

Copyright © 1908 by Adolf Furstner, Reviewed 1935, 1936. Copyright assigned 1943 to Boosey & Hawkes, Ltd. for all countries except Germany, Danzig, Italy, Portugal and USSR. Reprinted by permission of Boosey & Hawkes, Inc.

II. Parallel harmonies and the whole-tone scale.

Harmonize whole-tone scales using parallel harmonies.

        A. Major triad.
        B. Augmented triad.
        C. Major-minor seventh.
        D. Major ninth

Illustrations:

III. More parallel harmonies.

Complete the following passages using exact parallelism, i.e., harmonize each melodic note with a chord scored exactly as the first.

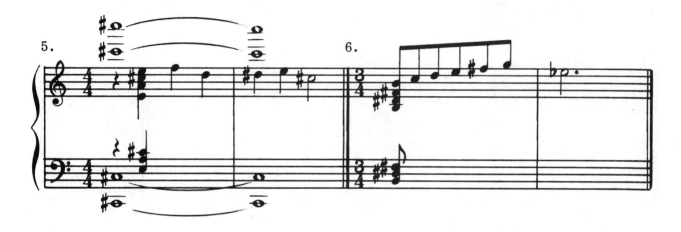

Project 44

Quartal Harmony

In conventional tertian harmony major and minor thirds are the basic intervals of chord structure. We recognize, however, that other intervals also have essential functions in this vocabulary—major or minor seconds appear in inverted seventh chords, tritones in diminished triads and various seventh chords, etc.

When the fundamental, generating function is assigned to the perfect fourth rather than the third the harmonic style is broadly classified as quartal. Other intervals are also present, but the overall effect of quartal harmony is characterized by its extensive use of perfect intervals.

In the passage quoted below the composer uses superimposed perfect fourths to evoke the sound of bells. The basic sonority consists of the perfect fourth projection, bb-eb-ab-db-gb, with the tones c and f occurring incidentally in the melodic line.

Ex. 44.1. Ravel, **La Vallee des cloches from "Miroirs"**

Used by permission of G. Schirmer, Inc.

When there is a maximum saturation of the most consonant perfect intervals in the harmony, there will necessarily be a minimum use of the most dissonant intervals of the minor second and tritone. This corollary is clearly exemplified in the next two examples. The basic tones in Ex. 44.2 are c#-f#-b-e-a. There are two adjacent fourth projections in Ex. 44.3, d-g-c-f and bb-eb-ab-db.

Ex. 44.2. Bartok, Violin Concerto No. 2

Copyright 1938 by Hawkes & Son (London) Ltd. Renewed 1965. Reprinted by permission of Boosey & Hawkes, Inc.

Ex. 44.3. Dello Joio, Suite for Piano

"Suite for Piano" by Norman Dello Joio. Copyright © 1945 by G. Schirmer, Inc. Used by permission.

The inversion of the perfect fourth triad results in the interval of a major second. Minor seconds and tritones may occasionally result from the melodic motion. Different fourth projections appear in each measure, or, as in Ex. 44.5, on each beat.

Ex. 44.4. Schuman, Three-Score Set.

"Three-Score Set" by William Schuman. Copyright © 1944 by G. Schirmer, Inc. Used by permission.

Ex. 44.5. Hindemith, "A Swan" from Six Chansons (piano reduction).

Used by permission of European American Music Distributors Corporation.

Quartal harmony is primarily defined by its emphasis on the perfect intervals. A second factor in its identity may be simply the spacing of the chords. Harmony may be classified as quartal, even though dissonant intervals are present, when the spacing is obviously in pairs of fourths.

Ex. 44.6. Bartok, "Fourths" (No. 131) from Mikrokosmos.

© copyright 1940 by Hawkes & Son (London) Ltd. Renewed 1967. Reprinted by permission of Boosey & Hawkes, Inc.

The essential harmonic vocabulary for this project includes the three and four-note chords derived from the projection of four perfect fourths. While the perfect intervals are most strongly characteristic, major and minor triads and minor seventh chords are not excluded. These chords may be differentiated from their more conventional counterparts by the spacing which emphasizes the perfect fourth.

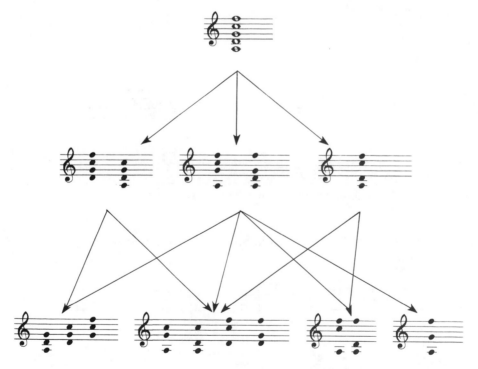

I. Quartal chords.

Play the following chords and sing each of the component tones in your own voice range. Secondly, play only the bass note and sing the other chord tones.

A. Three-note chords.

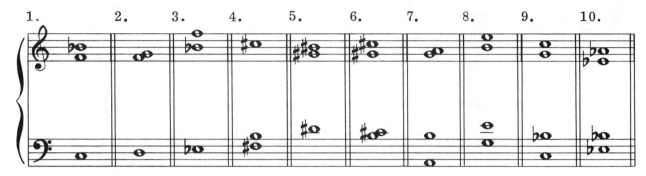

B. Four-note chords.

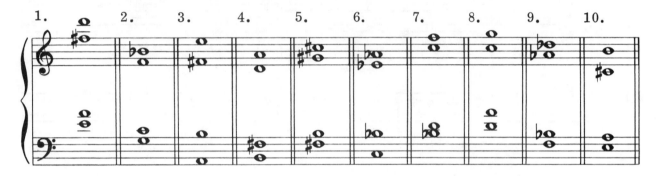

II. Phrases in quartal harmony.

A. Add inner parts to complete the following phrases in quartal harmony. A direct way to accomplish this is to add perfect fourths or fifth, above the bass and below the soprano, always avoiding combinations which contain minor seconds or tritones. Various other chord structures are also available; develop harmonizations which sound consistent and convincing. Parallel fourths and fifths are idiomatic in this style. Retaining one or two common tones between chords sometimes enhances the progression.

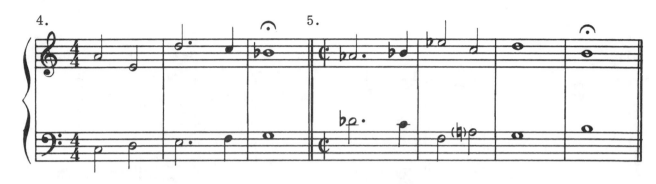

B. Play these phrases in various keys. Observe the use of fourth projections.

2.

3.

4.

C. Improvise keyboard continuations or completions for the following passages.

1.

Bichords

The combining of two conventional triads or seventh chords may produce very rich and colorful sonorities. The occurrence of bichords is often more apparent to the eye than to the ear. Unless the two chords involved are clearly differentiated by spacing, the several tones merge aurally into one complex sonority. Two triads are contained within any conventional seventh chord, but only a single chord structure, and a single root is perceived.

As the component triads are more separated in register, and when more nondiatonic tones are used (resulting in fewer common tones between the triads), the dual nature of these sonorities becomes increasingly apparent.

The bichord effect is present when two remotely related triads appear in close succession, even though all the tones are not sounded simultaneously. Remarkable examples of the bichord technique are to be found in the opera *Elektra* by Richard Strauss. The sound created by two minor triads with roots a tritone apart pervades the work. A second characteristic sonority results from the superposition of two major triads with roots a minor third apart—e-b♭, and b-f.

Ex. 45.1. Strauss, Elektra

Copyright © 1908 by Adolf Furstner, Renewed 1935, 1936. Copyright assigned 1943 to Boosey & Hawkes, Ltd. for all countries except Germany, Danzig, Italy, Portugal and USSR. Reprinted by permission of Boosey & Hawkes, Inc.

Ex. 45.2. Strauss, Elektra

Copyright © 1908 by Adolf Furstner, Renewed 1935, 1936. Copyright assigned 1943 to Boosey & Hawkes, Ltd. for all countries except Germany, Danzig, Italy, Portugal and USSR. Reprinted by permission of Boosey & Hawkes, Inc.

Ex. 45.3. Strauss, Elektra

Copyright © 1908 by Adolf Furstner, Renewed 1935, 1936. Copyright assigned 1943 to Boosey & Hawkes, Ltd. for all countries except Germany, Danzig, Italy, Portugal and USSR. Reprinted by permission of Boosey & Hawkes, Inc.

The bichord technique with both chords in close structure is especially suitable for keyboard performance. Observe the root relationships between the superimposed triads.

Ex. 45.4. Persichetti, Little Piano Book; No. 10, Prologue

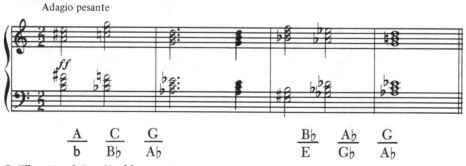

© Elkan-Vogel, Inc. Used by permission.

Ex. 45.5. Adler, *Gradus*; No. 20

C   A   F   G   D
A♭   E♭   D♭   C♭   F♯

From *Gradus: Book I* by Samuel Adler. Copyright © 1971 by Oxford University Press, Inc. Reprinted by permission.

Bichords combining two major triads may be classified in six groups, according to the basic interval distance between the chord roots. When the roots are separated by a perfect fourth, a major third, or a minor third, the triads will have one tone in common, and the bichord will have only five different tones. Triads with roots a major or minor second or tritone apart have no common tones.

I. Bichords.

Complete the following bichords by playing a different major triad with each hand. Use the lower given tone as a chord root and the upper tone as root, third, or fifth as indicated. (The first chord is notated, as an example.) After playing, sing the two chord roots and identify the basic interval between them.

A. Bass in close structure.

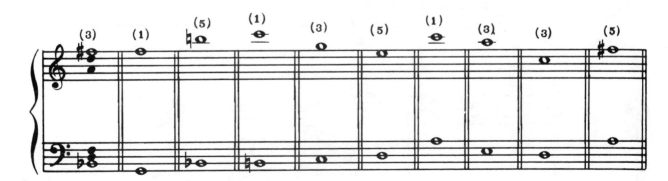

B. Bass in open structure.

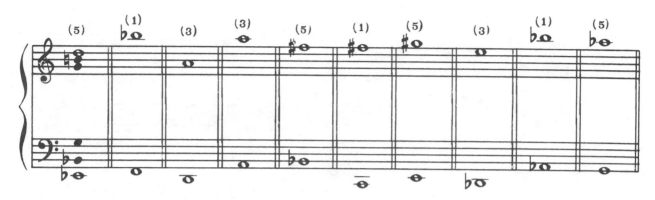

II. Phrases using bichords.

A. Complete the following passages by playing major triads in both hands. Continue the scoring suggested by the first bichord, using the given outer parts consistently as either roots, thirds, or fifths.

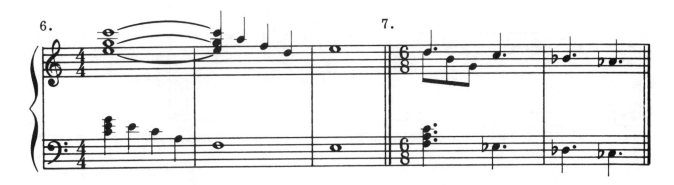

B. Play these phrases slowly and listen to the varied sonorities produced by the changing root relationships. Also use these passages as beginnings for further improvisations with bichords.

Serialism; Chords with Minor Seconds

The basic interval of the minor second occurs in traditional tonal music in only a few harmonic situations, such as IV⁷, V⁹ in minor, etc. Sonorities which include this interval have become quite commonplace in contemporary music, however, largely through the influence of serial techniques of composition.

There are only five different three-note combinations which contain minor seconds. These are illustrated below in the closest possible spacing. The second of these triads is the only one which includes both the tritone and the minor second. This chord has been referred to as the "Viennese fourth" because of its association with the Viennese composers, Berg, Schoenberg, and Webern. The third triad includes both the major the major and minor third—or, "split third". The last two triads, projections of major and minor seconds, might sometimes be classified as "tone clusters", depending on the context.

I. Minor second triads.

Play the following triads. Identify and sing the three basic intervals in any order, transposing the pitches by octaves to a comfortable voice range. Classify each triad according to its interval content.

For example:

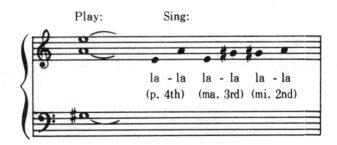

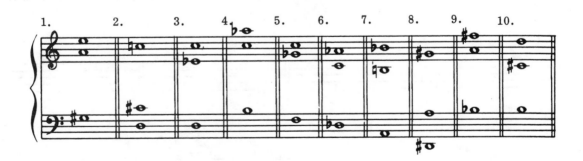

In serial composition all pitch relationships are derived from a predetermined series, or row, consisting of twelve (or fewer) different tones. Melodic and harmonic components are generated by using these tones in a consistent order or by transposing or manipulating them in any of three basic operations: inversion, retrograde, retrograde-inversion. Since a tone row is transposable to any level, it is more accurately regarded as a series of *intervals*, rather than of fixed pitches. While any interval relationships can be used in constructing a tone row, serial music typically avoids combinations having tertian, or tonal, implications. Consequently, the prominence of minor seconds (and, to a lesser degree, tritones) is usually a distinctive feature of the style.

II. *Manipulations of the five minor-second triads.*

Play, and/or sing, the three other versions of each three-note motive beginning on the given tones. Do not write out these solutions; rather, exercise your aural faculties by comparing the interval content of each motive with the original.

III. Six-tone series.

Sing the given six-tone series, using the piano for assistance if needed. Then use these series to improvise motives and melodic patterns. The series may be repeated at the same pitch level or transposed. Any of the tones may be displaced by one or more octaves. The prime and inverted forms are shown; read these backwards to produce retrograde and retrograde-inversion.

IV. Twelve-tone series.

A very useful tool in the study of serial music is a 12 x 12 matrix which displays the four row forms and the twelve transposition levels. The matrix is constructed with the prime forms in rows reading left to right and the retrograde forms reading right to left. The columns show the inversion (top to bottom) and the retrograde inversion (bottom to top). Each transposition is assigned an index number, 0 to 11. The prime and inverted forms are numbered according to their first notes, in ascending half steps. The index numbers for retrograde and retrograde inversion is the same as for their corresponding prime and inverted forms. A matrix for Schoenberg's *Suite for Piano*, Op. 25 is shown below.

Inversion

	0	1	3	9	2	11	4	10	7	8	5	6	
0	E	F	G	Db	Gb	Eb	Ab	D	B	C	A	Bb	0
11	Eb	E	Gb	C	F	D	G	Db	Bb	B	Ab	A	11
9	Db	D	E	Bb	Eb	C	F	B	Ab	A	Gb	G	9
3	G	Ab	Bb	E	A	Gb	B	F	D	Eb	C	Db	3
10	D	Eb	F	B	E	Db	Cb	C	A	Bb	G	Ab	10
1	F	Gb	Ab	D	G	E	A	Eb	C	Db	Bb	B	1
8	C	Db	Eb	A	D	B	E	Bb	G	Ab	F	Gb	8
2	Gb	G	A	Eb	Ab	F	Bb	E	Db	D	B	C	2
5	A	Bb	C	Gb	B	Ab	Db	G	E	F	D	Eb	5
4	Ab	A	B	F	Bb	G	C	Gb	Eb	E	Db	D	4
7	B	C	D	Ab	Db	Bb	Eb	A	Gb	G	E	F	7
6	Bb	B	Db	G	C	A	D	Ab	F	Gb	Eb	E	6

Prime (left side) — Retrograde (right side)

| 0 | 1 | 3 | 9 | 2 | 11 | 4 | 10 | 7 | 8 | 5 | 6 |

Retrograde—
Inversion

In the following excerpts the composer has used the prime form beginning on e and bb (P₀ and P₆) and the inverted form beginning on e (I₆).

Ex. 46.1. Schoenberg, Suite for Piano, Op. 25; Prelude

Used by permission of Belmont Music Publishers, Los Angeles, California 90049. Copyright 1968 by B. Schott's Söhne, Mainz, and Universal Edition AG, Vienna.

Ex. 46.2. Schoenberg, Suite for Piano, Op. 25; Trio

Used by permission of Belmont Music Publishers, Los Angeles, California 90049. Copyright 1968 by B. Schott's Söhne, Mainz, and Universal Edition AG, Vienna.

Ex. 46.3. Schoenberg, Suite for Piano Op. 25; Gigue

Used by permission of Belmont Music Publishers, Los Angeles, California 90049. Copyright 1968 by B. Schott's Söhne, Mainz, and Universal Edition AG, Vienna.

A matrix of the 12-tone series from Dallapiccola's "Quaderno Musicale di Annalibera" is given. Locate the transpositions and other manipulations of the series in the following excerpts.

	0	1	5	8	10	4	3	7	9	2	11	6	
0	B♭	B	E♭	F♯	A♭	D	D♭	F	G	C	A	E	0
11	A	B♭	D	F	G	D♭	C	E	F♯	B	A♭	E♭	11
7	F	F♯	B♭	D♭	E♭	A	A♭	C	D	G	E	B	7
4	D	E♭	G	B♭	C	F♯	F	A	B	E	D♭	A♭	4
2	C	D♭	F	A♭	B♭	E	E♭	G	A	D	B	G♭	2
8	F♯	G	B	D	E	B♭	A	D♭	E♭	A♭	F	C	8
9	G	A♭	C	E♭	F	B	B♭	D	E	A	F♯	D♭	9
5	E♭	E	A♭	B	D♭	G	F♯	B♭	C	F	D	A	5
3	D♭	D	F♯	A	B	F	E	A♭	B♭	E♭	C	G	3
10	A♭	A	D♭	E	F♯	C	B	E♭	F	B♭	G	D	10
1	B	C	E	G	A	E♭	D	F♯	A♭	D♭	B♭	F	1
6	E	F	A	C	D	A♭	G	B	D♭	G♭	E♭	B♭	6

| | 0 | 1 | 5 | 8 | 10 | 4 | 3 | 7 | 9 | 2 | 11 | 6 |

Ex. 46. 4. Dallapiccola, Quaderno Musicale di Annalibera; No. 8, Ritmi

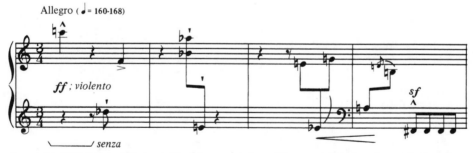

Copyright 1953 Edizioni Zerboni. Used by permission of Boosey & Hawkes, Inc. Sole Agents.

Ex. 46.5. Dallapiccola, Quaderno . . . ; No. 3, Contrapunctus Primus

Copyright 1953 Edizioni Zerboni. Used by permission of Boosey & Hawkes, Inc. Sole Agents.

Ex. 46.6. Dallapiccola, Quaderno . . . ; No. 11, Quartina

Copyright 1953 Edizioni Zerboni. Used by permission of Boosey & Hawkes, Inc. Sole Agents.

Ex. 46.7. Dallapiccola, Quaderno . . . ; No. 2, Accenti

Copyright 1953. Edizioni Zerboni. Used by permission of Boosey & Hawkes, Inc. Sole Agents.

Use the following twelve-tone rows for singing and experimentation at the keyboard.

Create your own twelve-tone rows and use them for further experimentation. Rows are not necessarily nontertian or even nontonal. Alban Berg's Violin Concerto is developed from the following series.

Generally it is desirable to have some variety of intervals in a row. Here is an extreme example containing all eleven different intervals, as measured in semitones.[1]

Arnold Schoenberg frequently used a particular type of row in which the first six tones, when inverted at the fifth below, produced the six remaining tones. The following row is the basis for his Fourth String Quartet, Op. 37.

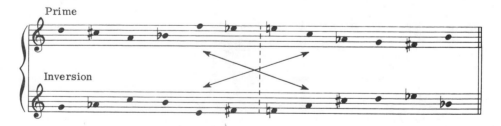

[1]This row is derived from the "Mother Chord," credited to Fritz Klein and discussed by Nicolas Slonimsky in his *Thesaurus of Scales and Melodic Patterns*, Coleman-Ross Co., 1947.

Review and Survey of Other Harmonic Techniques

In the last unit we have investigated various chromatic and twentieth-century harmonic practices. Some of these have utilized traditional chord structures in special ways, while others were based on distinctive chord vocabularies. Practices in the former category are defined principally by *context* and include additional uses of the augmented sixth, enharmonic modulation, and harmonic sequence. Parallel harmony, too, is primarily a technique of applying conventional sonorities in a nonfunctional manner, although the resultant horizontal relationships often do not conform to any previous style. Modal harmony uses traditional triads, but with root relationships that are distinguishable from conventional tonality.

Other styles are defined principally by *content,* i.e., a unique, definable melodic-harmonic vocabulary. Several such vocabularies have been suggested here, including the resources of the whole-tone scale, quartal harmony, bichords, and chords with minor seconds. Ninths and other extended tertian chords do not comprise a complete vocabulary in themselves, but serve to enrich several other styles.

Jazz harmony does not fit easily into either category. Most of the harmonic structures idiomatic to jazz can be found in other styles, such as whole-tone chords and bichords. So *context* may be the more definitive factor for this style. There are, however, some chords that suggest jazz derivation even when heard singularly—augmented ninths and elevenths, for example—so perhaps harmonic *content* is also partially definitive.

Play and listen to each of the following chords. Sing the chord tones or roots. Consider possible derivations or harmonic categories for each. These chords all relate to preceding discussions of jazz harmony, the whole-tone scale, quartal harmony, bichords, and chords with minor seconds.

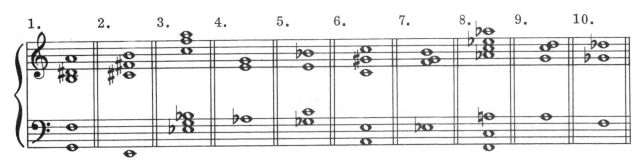

Survey of Other Harmonic Techniques

The seven common modal scales use seven different tones and include five whole steps and two half steps. There are two additional sets, with seven scales in each, which have these same characteristics. A representative scale from each set is shown. These are the symmetrical versions, or modes, of each set, equivalent to the Dorian of the conventional modes. Each can be inverted to form six other modes. The distance between scale degrees is measured in semitones.[1]

One of the modes from this first set has attracted particular attention. It is sometimes called the "mixed mode scale," because of its Lydian fourth and Mixolydian seventh, and sometimes the "overtone scale" because its tones conform to an acoustical partial series.

Another interesting scale contains eight different tones in alternating whole and half steps. It was perhaps first used by Rimsky-Korsakov, but has been employed by many other composers, including Scriabin and Bartok. It is referred to as the octatonic scale or diminished seventh scale.

[1]See Appendix 1 for graphic representations of these and other scales.

A scale with two augmented seconds is variously termed the Hungarian or Gypsy scale. It is also sometimes used to evoke Indian ragas.

Verdi's "enigmatic" scale also includes an augmented second. There are half steps above and below the tonic, while the interior of the scale emphasizes whole tones.

Scale possibilities seem almost infinite. You may want to experiment with some of the scales mentioned here or invent your own pitch system. Try dividing the twelve-semitone octave into various divisions of from one to four semitones. Or divide two octaves into three parts, three octaves into four, etc., and then further subdivide these fractions. As an example, here is a nine-tone scale that was originated by dividing two octaves into three parts, eight semitones in size.

Chords may be constructed by similar processes. Many of the available chords containing up to four different tones have been included in this book, as well as some five- and six-tone chords.

There is one chord of particular historical interest which does not fit comfortably into any of our harmonic categories. It is called the "Mystic" or "Prometheus" chord and was used extensively by Scriabin.

Various rationales have been advanced to explain its structure. It has often been classified as quartal, for obvious reasons. The chord tones conform to the overtone scale, and, with the exception of the note 'a,' they also fit into a whole-tone scale. The weight of the major thirds, major seconds, and tritones supports the idea of a whole-tone derivation.

Recent theoretical studies have contributed significantly toward an understanding of Scriabin's unique harmonic style.[2] The analytical system is complex, generally originating with the tritone, and proceeding through extensions including the French sixth, whole-tone scale, and minor third scale.

[2]See Faubion Bowers, *The New Scriabin, Enigma and Answers* (New York: St. Martin's Press, 1973).

It will be of interest to experiment at the keyboard with this chord, playing it in various transpositions and inversions. The "Mystic" chord is a good representative of Scriabin's later harmonic style, but it is by no means his only contribution. A few of his many other colorful harmonies, extracted and reduced from his piano sonatas, are illustrated below.

"Tone clusters" is the term used by Henry Cowell to describe the large chords of superimposed major and minor seconds which he employed in his compositions as early as 1912. Such chords use consecutive piano keys and may span intervals ranging in size from a third to several octaves. On the piano they may be played with flat fingers or the side of the hand, the fist, or one or both forearms, as well as with the fingertips. Some sample notations follow. A natural sign indicates that only the white keys are included in the cluster, a sharp or flat indicates a black key cluster, while the absence of any accidental means that all intervening keys, black and white, are to be played. Try playing the following clusters at various dynamic levels, with and without pedal.

Clusters can also be more specifically notated. Several combinations of three, four, and five tones are illustrated. Chords of this type have been referred to as secundal harmony. Try singing the component tones as you play these. Can such chords be aurally distinguished from one another?

When applied to orchestral music the large tone clusters may be called "sound mass." Many instruments sound in consecutive half steps, either on sustained pitches or with interweaving melodic motion. An extension of this technique leads beyond tempered tuning into various generalizations of pitch or specified microtones.

Tone clusters may create very thick musical textures. At the opposite extreme on the gamut of densities is a transparent, delicate texture described as "pointillism." The melodic lines consist of widely spaced pitches, characteristically in short note values. The style is most often associated with serial organizations. Nicolas Slonimsky's "grandmother chord" contains twelve different tones and eleven symmetrically invertible intervals.[3] A pointillistic melody derived from this chord has c^1 as a center axis.

In recent years composers have developed new ways of creating musical sounds on the piano. The techniques include modifying the strings and playing directly on the strings in various ways.

A "prepared piano" is one in which various objects have been placed on or between the strings to alter the sounds. Small wood, metal, rubber, or plastic items may be used, with each having a potentialy different effect on the tone quality. Experiment by placing rubber erasers or faucet washers between the strings at different locations and listening to the resultant timbres. Select and prepare perhaps five or six notes and compose or improvise a short piece. These string sounds might be accompanied by drumlike rhythmic effects created by tapping on the wood surfaces of the piano case.

Another technique is to silently depress some piano keys with one hand while strumming across the associated strings with the other. Holding down certain keys lifts the dampers off the strings so those tones will ring while the others are suppressed. Try this with several harmonic styles—tertian, whole-tone, quartal, clusters, etc.

A variety of colorful sounds can also be produced inside the piano by rubbing the strings lengthwise with fingers of fingernails and by plucking or striking strings with the hand or a soft beater. Harmonics can be produced by lightly touching a string at a nodal point—a fractional division of its total vibrating length, one-half, one-third, etc. These techniques may require two performers, one playing inside the piano, the other manipulating keys and pedals.

We have considered the compositional technique of serialism in which pitches are used according to a predetermined scheme of rotation. Other musical parameters may be subjected to similar serialized controls. A rhythmic series can be constructed by specifying a certain order of note values or groupings or notes. Dynamics, articulation, registers, instruments, and densities are other musical components that have been serialized. The procedure is known as "total organization." The totality of such controls, however, should be taken as a relative, rather than an absolute concept. While pitch serialization most frequently includes twelve factors in a row, other serialized parameters usually

[3]The grandmother chord was invented by Slonimsky on February 13, 1938. See his *Thesaurus of Scales and Melodic Patterns,* Coleman-Ross Co., 1947.

operate on shorter series. The score of a work composed in this way is necessarily very detailed in its specifications. The resulting performance is highly predictable—although there may be extreme demands upon the skills of the performer—and there should be little variance between several presentations of the same work.

While some composers have striven to increase their control over the creation and performance of their work, others have explored the divergent approach of relinquishing some of their traditional prerogatives. This may take the form of leaving some of the initial creative choices to chance or of assigning more creative responsibility to the performer by providing only generalized instructions.

Music composed by chance or random methods is called aleatoric music. Choices of pitches or rhythms, or any other musical element, may be decided by tossing a coin, rolling dice, etc. The entire composition may be developed in this way or the composer may reserve some of the choices for himself and leave others to chance. A simple experiment would be to assign a pitch to each of the six numbers on a die, notate the results of a few throws, and form these pitches into a melody. Another series of throws could produce note values, another, accompanying chords, etc.

The idea of a composer transmitting nonspecific performance instructions has many applications. Even conventional notation is not completely explicit and leaves much to the performer's discretion. In indeterminate music more of the decisions are transferred from composer to performer. The results are unpredictable in varying degrees. Some avant-garde scores have no musical notation at all, but perhaps only sketches, diagrams, or pictures. Others combine conventional and graphic notation. Standardization has not yet been achieved with this type of notation, so it is usually necessary to include interpretative directions in the score.

Symmetrical Sonorities

Symmetry in groups of musical tones results when they are in a balanced or equidistant relationship, for instance, when a center division would create two like and equal parts. The sonorities that divide an octave into equal parts have this quality. Also, pairs of chords or scales that form mirror images, or palindromes, are symmetrical.

These relationships can be demonstrated visually by inscribing figures within a circle of fifths.

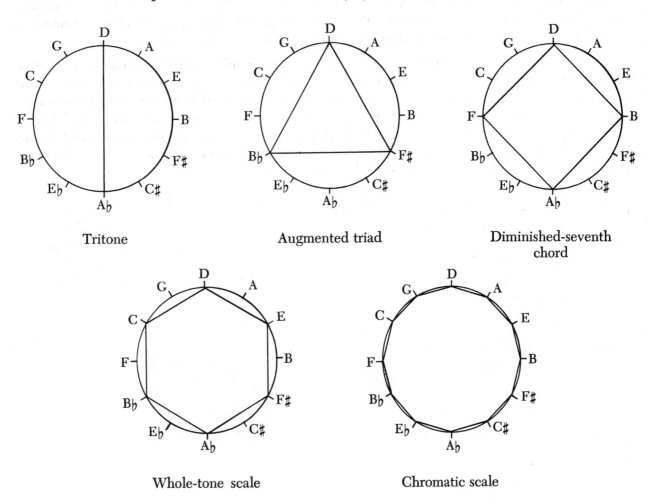

Tritone	Augmented triad	Diminished-seventh chord

Whole-tone scale	Chromatic scale

The inscribed figures could be rotated to indicate transpositions. There are six possible positions for the line that represents the tritone, so there are six available, mutually exclusive tritones. The same procedure shows that there are four mutually exclusive augmented triads, three diminished seventh chords, two whole-tone scales, and one chromatic scale.

Theorists have often observed that the minor triad is a mirror of the major. Likewise, the diminished-minor seventh mirrors the major-minor seventh.

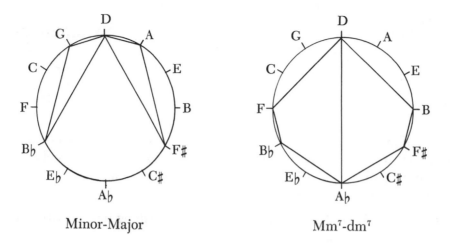

Minor-Major   Mm⁷-dm⁷

The two tetrachords of the Dorian mode are in a mirror relationship. The complete Dorian mode, represented here with the note 'd' as final, includes no accidentals and occupies the top half of our circle.

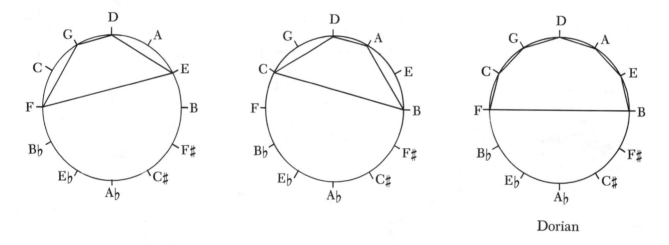

Dorian

The other conventional modes are shown in their mirror pairs.

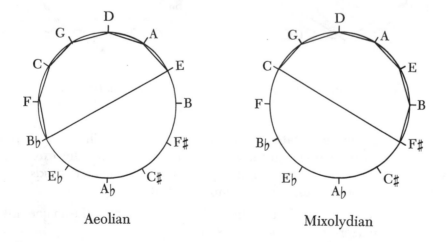

Aeolian   Mixolydian

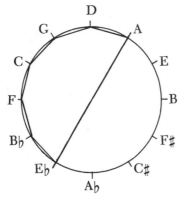

Phrygian

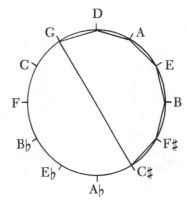

Ionian

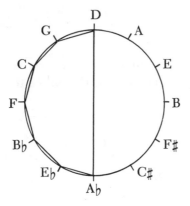

Locrian

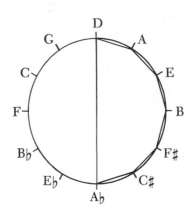

Lydian

The symmetrical mode of two other seven-mode sets are illustrated below, followed by their divisions into two equal tetrachords. Each of these modes can be inverted to form six additional scales. These six scales will form mirror pairs similar to the conventional modes.

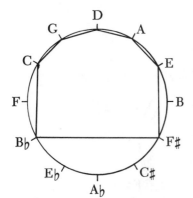

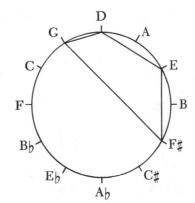

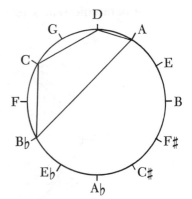

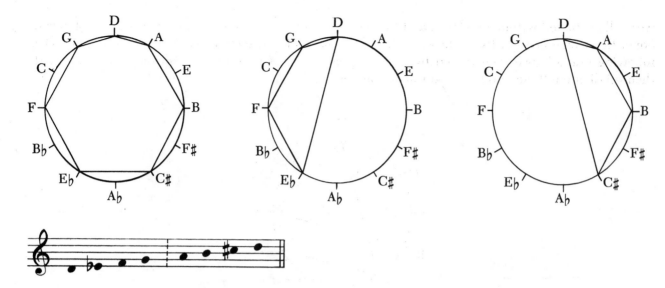

Sonorities derived from those dividing an octave equally may have similarly symmetrical forms. For instance, here are the three four-note chords which occur within the whole-tone scale.

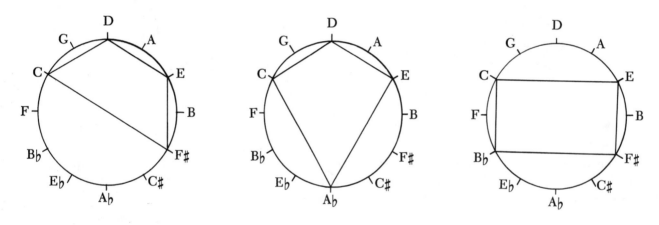

The octatonic scales relate to the diminished seventh chord.

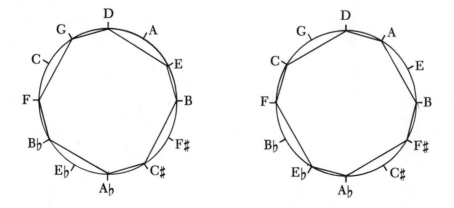

Any combination of tones, whether symmetrical or not, can be represented in this way, and the procedure can also be used to generate or examine new sonorities. The patterns we have illustrated were all contained within an octave, and the representations were simple, closed geometric figures. Sonorities which close at two octaves, rather than one, will create more complex visual designs. The following example was constructed by first dividing two octaves into three eight-semitone units, and then subdividing these into five- and three-semitone units.

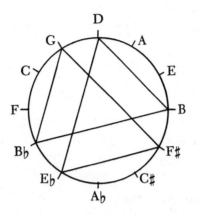

Selected References to Bach Chorale Harmonizations

The chorale harmonizations of J. S. Bach comprise the most significant body of music literature set in a consistent four-voice texture.[1] They provide difficult, but rewarding, models for study and emulation. The rich harmonic language and imaginative use of nonharmonic material challenge the perception and insight of the analyst.

It is instructive to study various specific techniques in these harmonizations. In the case of chords one might consider the surrounding harmonies, the treatment of dissonance and the interrelationships of harmony and melody. The chorale references that follow are by no means comprehensive, but illustrate clear and typical applications of certain chords. The chorale number appears first, followed by the phrase in which the chord appears.

I. Diatonic seventh chords. References to the dominant seventh and the leading-tone seventh in minor are not included here. These chords are so versatile and so frequent in their use as to almost defy meaningful generalization. They appear in all inversions and with all types of preparation for the chord seventh.

   A. The leading-tone seventh in major keys. This chord is not common in the Bach harmonizations. In these passages it appears as a double passing-tone figure.
       53, 3
       121, 1
       324, 4

   B. The subdominant seventh in major and minor.

Root position	1st inversion	3rd inversion
2, 6	147, 3	316, 4
72, 1	214, 9	
81, 1		
110, 5		
292, 5		

   C. The submediant seventh in major.

       26, 2
       39, 2

       84, 5
       112, 2

       109, 3

   D. The submediant seventh in minor.

       145, 3
       266, 5

       346, 1

---

[1]The most thorough study of the Bach chorales appears in McHose, *The Contrapuntal Harmonic Technique of the 18th Century* (New York: Appleton-Century-Crofts, 1947). Extensive chorale references are included.

E. The mediant seventh in major.

26, 2

213, 1

95, 2

F. The tonic seventh in major.

12, 1

191, 5

II. Secondary dominants.

A. V^7 of V—altered ii^7.

Major keys	Minor keys
12, 2	21, 2
107, 10	59, last
115, 3 & 5	324, last
156, 4	356, 6
217, 4	
265, 5	
89, 1	
118, 6	
238, 2	

B. vii^{o7o} of V (diminished)—altered IV^7.

Major keys	Minor keys
59, 2	9, 3
84, 6	26, 4
107, 9	47, last
340, 4	87, 2
	94, 5
	167, 4

C. vii^{o7} of V (diminished-minor)—altered IV^7.

Major keys

67, 6

121, 5

216, 8

275, last

338, 2

D. V of V—altered ii.

4, last

12, 3

146, 2

293, 3

E. vii^o of V—altered IV.

50, 2

68, 1

200, 1

275, 2

F. V^7 of IV in major—altered I^7.

   51, last
   223, last
   1, 4
   222, 1
   351, 1

   6, 1
   11, 1
   108, last
   231, 1
   275, last

   46, 2
   147, 1

G. V^7 and vii^{o7o} of iv in minor—altered i^7 and III^7.

   9, 4
   210, 6
   252, 8 (2)

   203, 1
   8, 1

   3, 5
   300, 1

H. Secondary dominants of ii in major.

   276, last
   284, 5
   152, 4
   217, 3
   303, 3

   67, last
   252, last
   322, 4

   139, 2

   156, 3
   234, 3

I. Secondary dominants of vi in major.

   217, 3
   366, 4

   84, 2
   156, 3
   224, 1
   252, 7
   268, 2

   92, 4
   151, 1

24, 2
58, 7
176, 3

III.   Borrowed chords in major keys.

310, last

59, 2
139, 1
279, last
341, 3

6, last
216, 8

267, 5

89, 3
216, 4
322, 1

IV.   The Neapolitan-sixth and augmented sixth chords.

262, 2

19, 1
146, 2
216, 8
300, 4
340, 5

The Chopin Mazurkas: A Thesaurus of Chromatic Harmony

This collection provides a convenient and accessible resource for the study of various chromatic procedures. The texture is relatively clear and the technical requirements moderate, so they are within the performance abilities of many student pianists. The chromaticism, while frequently very striking, is quite concise and is firmly buttressed within areas of unambiguous tonality.

I. Enharmonic modulation.

   A. Through the augmented sixth. These modulations move up or down a half step, up a major third, or a tritone.

Opus & Number	Measure
7, 2	13
24, 1	48
24, 2	57
30, 2	20 & 28
30, 3	33
33, 4	17 & 63
56, 1	34 & 44
56, 3	49 & 57 & 66
59, 1	8
59, 3	96
68, 4	19

   B. Through the diminished seventh.

7, 4	36
17, 3	23
30, 3	33
56, 3	136

   C. Other enharmonic modulations and relationships.

24, 4	68
56, 1	77
59, 1	14
63, 1	24
63, 3	32 & 48
68, 4	14

II. Harmonic sequence. These passages imply modulation to the extent that new, transient key centers are established.

6, 1	5
7, 2	21
17, 1	15

17, 4	9 & 108
24, 3	25
30, 2	25
30, 4	129
50, 3	157
56, 1	23
56, 2	37
56, 3	135 & 184
59, 2	85
59, 3	65
67, 2	21
68, 4	32

III. Neapolitan chords and/or key relationships.

7, 4	13
17, 2	39
30, 3	34
30, 4	23
33, 4	209
59, 3	131
63, 1	22
63, 2	7

IV. Other materials.

A. Dominant function augmented sixths.

17, 4	118
56, 3	80
63, 1	23

B. Foreign modulation to keys a third apart.

33, 2	49
41, 3	15 & 35

C. Special scales.

6, 2	1
24, 2	5
41, 1	1
68, 2	1

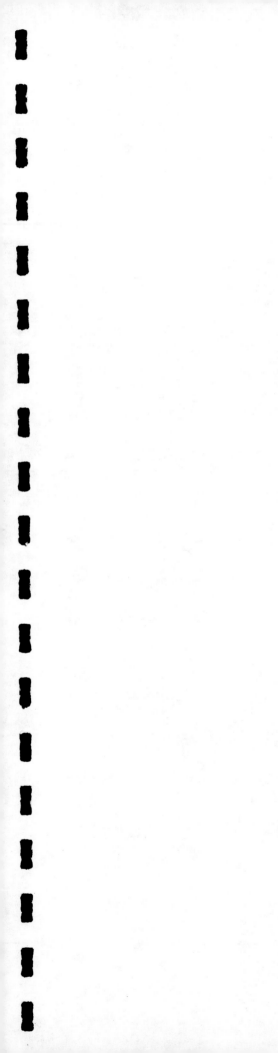